Willa Marsh

Willa Marsh is the pseudonym of Marcia Willett, author
of several novels that have been published with great
success by Headline. She originally studied dance at The
Maddocks School of Dancing and spent her early career
teaching ballet and ballroom dancing at her sister's dance
academy. In 1982 her husband was commissioned to
write a book on sailing and the couple moved on board
their ketch for twelve months, during which time she
started to write. Willa Marsh lives with her husband and
their two Newfoundland dogs in a small Devon village on
the edge of Dartmoor.

Willa Marsh's previous novel, AMY WINGATE'S
JOURNAL, is also available from Sceptre.

SCEPTRE

Facing
The
Music

WILLA MARSH

SCEPTRE

Copyright © 1997 Marcia Willett

First published in 1997 by Hodder and Stoughton
First published in paperback in 1998 by Hodder and Stoughton
A division of Hodder Headline PLC
A Sceptre Paperback

The right of Marcia Willett to be identified as the Author of
the Work has been asserted by her in accordance with the
Copyright, Designs and Patents Act 1988.

10 9 8 7 6 5 4 3 2 1

A CIP catalogue record for this title is available
from the British Library.

ISBN 0 340 67477 6

Printed and bound in Great Britain by
Clays Ltd, St Ives plc

Hodder and Stoughton
A division of Hodder Headline PLC
338 Euston Road
London NW1 3BH

To Carrye

1

I saw a rook today, with a straw in its beak, and I was visited by an inexplicable, unnamed longing; the kind of poignant yearning that one associates with the anguish of youth rather than with the sensible placidity of middle age. I watched the rook for a moment as it wheeled, black against a turbulent sky – storm-grey clouds torn apart to reveal patches of pure tender blue – and saw it drop into the bare branches of a stand of tall oaks in which the colony of rooks makes its home.

It must have been the arrival of Vanessa's letter which put me in this mood for reminiscence. Why else should the sight of a nesting rook cause me to think of Elizabeth Ferrars? Her voice, clipped and cool, echoes in my ears;

'I hate the autumn. It's so depressing with the nights drawing in and winter ahead. I'm a spring person, Marchant.' She always called me by my surname. 'I need the promise of renewal and fresh hope. I love the early primroses and lambs bleating and the long light evenings. You wait. You'll feel just the same when you're older.'

'But Christmas!' I'd insisted, the joys of autumn having been so summarily dismissed. 'Surely the thought of Christmas . . .?'

Her face closed against me, the light dying out of her

eyes. 'I hate Christmas!' she said bleakly and turned back to her work.

Even now, nearly twenty-five years on, I burn with shame as I remember.

I was a child, I tell myself, an ignorant naive girl of barely nineteen.

Today, though, I am unable to push the uncomfortable memories aside so easily and the past comes a little closer, impinging on the present, reminding me . . .

I walk on quickly, bending my head against a quick patter of rain, hurrying in through the gate and up the narrow brick path. Our cottage, next to the church, is a squat comfortable shape. It grows out of the very ground and I love its uneven floors and unexpected turns and twists. We moved here nearly eight years ago, after our darling ten-year-old daughter was killed in a school minibus accident. The fact that it had taken us so many years to conceive a child made it even more desperately difficult to come to terms with our loss. She was so very precious to us. I seriously wondered if James might die of grief; he became so withdrawn, so silent. He started to stay later at the office hoping, no doubt, that work would assuage his overwhelming misery.

To combat the thrust of pain which still accompanies each memory of Sarah's death, I concentrate on Vanessa's letter. It is years now since we met but we have always stayed in touch. She lives in some remote, luxurious watering place which I have promised I shall visit but never do.

'. . . Alex wants to return to the land of his fathers, don't ask me why, darling! He could take the pick of a dozen jobs out here but he's being thoroughly tiresome! He's got himself a university place to do a post-graduate course and is coming over for an interview. I've given in. I made him promise to try things out here for a year but I might as well have saved my breath. You'll put him up, won't you darling? Help him get settled and so on. I know you'll like him. He's very like his father – but you'll see that when you meet him . . .'

I put the letter back on the table thoughtfully. Vanessa and Tony; how beautiful they were, how glamorous and exciting to my innocent eager eyes. I remember Vanessa as I first saw her, working in the boutique on the third floor at Winslow's, where her beauty and style shone out unmistakably. Whatever was she doing there? As I go into my low-beamed sitting room, and kneel to put a match to the fire, I am seeing her as she was then. I settle myself, resting against my chair; watching the flames take hold, travelling back in time.

It was my father who found me the job in the large department store in our neighbouring university town. He feared that, left to myself, I should idle my time away making little or no effort to find the work that he declared was necessary to give me self-esteem and a sense of purpose. He added that he had no intention of supporting me and that it would do me good to earn my own money instead of spending his. He would drone on for some time in this fashion whilst my mother, smiling vaguely, dreamily contemplated a world other than ours. She was a painter; he was an industrialist. It did not occur to me to engage my mother in serious conversation regarding my future. Even during my earliest years she had lived beyond my childhood world. She was special, talented, almost magical. My father adored her, surrounding her in a cloud of mystique, whilst I watched from an awed, wondering distance. A bedtime story read by my mother was a tremendous treat; I sat quiet as a mouse in my little bed and never contradicted as I did when my father read to me. I watched her hands holding the book, the long fingers turning the pages, her lips as they moved. It was she who fascinated – not the story.

As I grew, it seemed that she receded even further from me and, as she became more famous and required more protection from the press, from her fans, from her own occasional moods of depression, so it became more impossible to establish the contact for which I longed. *She* had no such need.

'How should *I* know?' she would say helplessly, should I attempt to seek advice. 'Speak to your father . . .' and off she would go, drifting away across the lawn to her studio.

'Don't bother your mother,' my father would say, harassed and anxious. 'What about a secretarial course? Or cooking . . .?'

I had no desire to be either a secretary or a cook and told him so. I wanted to live in a romantic dream, waiting for a knight in shining armour – or the modern equivalent – to come riding up the gravelled drive and whisk me off into the land of Happy Ever After.

It was on a Sunday morning, after his round of golf, that my father broke the news to me. Somehow the subject of my lack of employment had arisen and his partner, the managing director of the department store, suggested that I might like to train to be a buyer. I was to make an appointment to see him.

I protested, naturally. My mother, appealed to by both of us, looked faintly alarmed.

'"Work in a shop"?' She repeated my indignant phrase, *almost* concerned – but not overwhelmingly so – and making an attempt to concentrate. 'A shop? What shop? Surely . . .?'

She paused; the unspoken reproach hanging in the air. My father, glaring at me, tried to make things clearer.

'She is to be a buyer,' he said impressively, carving the wafer-thin slices of meat of which my mother approved.

She hated anything coarse or large; a loaded plate was anathema to her.

'But,' her pale brow wrinkled, 'if she is to work in a shop, surely she will be a "seller".'

We were taken aback by this mild essay into humour but my father was not to be distracted.

'It is not just a "shop",' he told her. 'Good heavens, Maria! You have your lunch there, whenever you go to town. All our friends have accounts at Winslow's. It's like Harrods. David is suggesting that she should be trained in the china and glass department. She will be working with beautiful objects.'

My mother looked at me compassionately, shrugging a little to indicate her helplessnesss, and I could see that her brief moment of partisanship was over. I wondered, not for the first time, if she were disappointed that I was so obviously my father's daughter. He was broad, stocky, fair, with an open expression and inky blue eyes. I was as like him as it is possible for a girl of eighteen to resemble a man in his mid-forties. Our colouring was very English; had we been dogs it would have been described as wheaten.

My mother was ivory-skinned with blue-black hair. I envied her her bones, her slenderness, her elegance, more than I coveted her skill with a paintbrush. It was long since I had given up trying to impress her or win her approval. It was Alma, the woman who walked up daily from the village to attend to the smooth running of the house, to whom I took my minor victories and major defeats. It was Alma, with her red-brown hair and eyes to match, who encouraged, sympathised, rejoiced, and it was she who reconciled me to my new position.

'Sounds grand,' she said. 'just grand. Winslow's! Well.'

I looked to see if she were humouring me but Alma rarely dissembled. It was because of this that I knew I could trust her. It never occurred to me that Alma had never set foot inside the exclusive store which catered for the wealthy and was located in the fashionable and élitist part of the town. I suspect now that, knowing her influence with me, my father had warned her to be positive. She was just as keen as he was to see me gainfully employed. As a devout Methodist she believed firmly in 'Satan finds . . .'

'I'm to start in Haberdashery,' I told her, 'just to get the feel of things for a month or two. Then I begin my training with Mrs Ferrars in the china and glass department. I could finish up doing the whole of the buying for the department. I wouldn't be selling at all. I shall go to London to do the buying, of course.'

I tried out these grand phrases on her, repeating them parrot-like, as David Eastwell had tried them out on me in his spacious office on the top floor. I guessed that he had heard of my intransigence and he was persuasive and kindly. I promised that I would give it a try and my father's relief was so great that he muttered something about a little car, should I stick at it. I recognised a bribe when I saw one and it was this, allied with Alma's encouragement, which brought me to the starting post.

Even for those days I was unusually naive. Because of my mother's reclusive tendencies and the sacredness with which my father regarded her work, I was not encouraged to have friends to stay. I had been a weekly boarder at a private school some miles away and so was neither fish, flesh nor good red herring. I was an outsider both at school – where the majority of pupils boarded – and at home – where I was discouraged from making friendships with 'the village' – and I had no good friends in either place.

'Party?' my mother would ask, already distressed by the mere suggestion. 'Why should you want a party? You are not a child.'

I forbore to point out that, even as a child, I had not been
allowed birthday parties.

'I just thought it might be fun,' I would mutter. 'The girls
at school . . .'

'Oh . . .' The girls at school, who might have been more
forthcoming had I invited them to my home, were dismissed
by a flick of the wrist and an impatient shake of the head. It
implied that only someone as inadequate as I would need
the support and companionship of people of my own age.
I resorted to books and to Alma to learn of the world so it
is not strange that I had a fairly unrealistic view of it.

Now, I imagine, it would be impossible for a young girl to
be as ignorant as I was then and, as I stare into the heart of
the fire, I try to remember those early days at Winslow's.

It never occurred to me that any of the members of staff
would know of my connection with David Eastwell. After
all, I barely knew him and I was too unversed in the power
struggle of the working world to know about pulling rank.
This was just as well. The news had already trickled down
from the top floor and, although I had no idea of it, my
fellow workers were preparing to resent me. It is clear,
looking back, that David Eastwell had deemed it best to
let me fend for myself. On the appointed Monday morning
I went in through the staff entrance and, with trepidation,
presented myself at the personnel manager's office. I had
been told to report at nine thirty and, having shaken my
hand and welcomed me to Winslow's, he sent for the buyer
of the haberdashery department. Miss Tremlett, he told me
as we awaited her arrival, was a long-established, faithful
servant of whom the company was very proud. She was a
short wiry woman with snow-white hair and very brown
eyes. Her manner to him was at once servile and confident
and the personnel manager, who was a good twenty years
younger than she was, spoke to her with deference.

I realise now that I had no idea of hierarchy, no respect for position. As we descended the stairs together I spoke to her with an easy friendliness which she at once repulsed. Her answers were brief and sarcastic and I was puzzled. With hindsight I can imagine her difficulty. She had worked for Winslow's all her life, moving between the three big branches, as she climbed the ladder from sales assistant to buyer. She was very aware of her own position and claimed her privileges ostentatiously: eating in the store's big restaurant; entering and leaving by one of the main doors; wearing her own choice of colour and style of clothes. She was respected, feared even, and here was I, a new girl, lowliest of the low, chatting to her as if I were her equal. Had I not been a friend of the MD I know she would have snubbed me utterly; as it was she tried to put me in my place without being too unkind lest I might be tempted to rush off, telling tales.

I had no idea of this then; nor was there time to brood on it. We were descending the last few steps to the ground floor department and I was aware of the attention we were receiving. Eyes: darting, staring, glancing, flicking, so that I felt that I was physically brushed by light, feathery blows. Her colour high, Miss Tremlett marched across to the haberdashery department and bustled behind the glass counter. I followed her.

A middle-aged woman and two girls awaited us. I was aware of their avid interest as she introduced me. Mrs Bateman was her second-in-command, a friendly middle-aged woman, who was in charge of scarves, costume jewellery, gloves and handkerchiefs. Miss Clarke, the taller and older of the two girls, was next in the hierarchy and had the rest of the haberdashery under her care. Miss Blake was a mere dogsbody.

The four glass counters, with the goods displayed in the cases beneath, were set in a huge square in the centre of which a wooden erection contained drawer upon drawer of the items which we were to sell. Mrs Bateman regularly changed the display within three of the glass cases but under the haberdashery counter were drawers of elastic, ribbon, zips, buttons and so on which were rarely altered except to be dusted and replenished.

Miss Tremlett, it appeared, could never be still. Her hands were always busy; twitching at the displays upon the counter, checking drawers for tidiness, questing for dust. A quick jab in one's ribs with a sharp elbow as she hurried past; bony fingers poked in one's back if a customer were to be spied approaching; a frustrated, impatient sigh if she came upon any of us standing still; all these outward manifestations of her authority made us dislike her. From the beginning it was my fate to annoy her.

Having introduced me and made Carol Clarke responsible for my education, she glanced at her watch. She sighed and tutted simultaneously, a habit she had, and glared at me.

'It's after ten o'clock' she announced irritably. 'You had better go to coffee, Miss Marchant.'

I stared at her in surprise. 'Go for coffee?' I repeated. 'At ten o'clock? It isn't coffee time.'

She flushed a dark unbecoming puce and I saw the two younger girls nudge each other with a kind of involuntary horror as she turned to pluck distractedly at a display of silk scarves, speaking to me with her face turned away.

'Whilst you are employed at Winslow's it is, Miss Marchant. As the most junior member of this department you will take first break. Coffee at ten, lunch at twelve, tea at three.'

'Lunch at twelve?' I was always a slow learner. 'I shan't be hungry.'

She looked at me then with a sharp look, assessing how much insolence was calculated in my reply. When she saw that I was merely distressed her expression became sarcastic.

'I deeply regret that we shall be inconveniencing you,' she said acidly. 'You will take early break today, Miss Blake and show Miss Marchant to the staff canteen. You have fifteen minutes for coffee of which you have already wasted three.'

I looked at Miss Blake – I later learned that she, too, was Carol – who jerked her head resentfully, implying that I should follow her.

'Well? Go on! Go on!' Miss Tremlett pushed me after her, she simply couldn't bear slowness or stupidity, and I trailed behind Carol Blake until we reached the staircase.

'Sorry,' I said, feeling that some apology was called for since this was not her usual coffee time.

She shrugged but didn't speak. I studied her covertly. She was as small and pale as the other Carol was tall and dark; Big Carol and Little Carol. I felt her antagonism towards me although I couldn't understand it and our exchanges during that first coffee break were very monosyllabic. We were both aware that we were attracting attention and, whilst I thought that it was simply the interest which a new girl arouses, my guess is that she feared that her friends might think she was trying to curry favour with me. After an uneasy beginning we became friends but there were one or two alarms and excursions first . . . .

The logs fall apart with a shower of sparks and I jump back, pushing the chair across the carpet. To my surprise I see that it is nearly dark and I glance hastily at my watch. James will be home soon and there is the supper to prepare.

2

'I had a letter from Vanessa today' The words tremble on my lips but I do not speak them. Why not? Some instinct – developed over all these years of marriage – warns me that this is not the moment. James is coping with a great deal of pressure at the office – mainly due to the loss of a valuable client – and is, meanwhile, trying to keep the peace between his older brother and his elderly father who are at odds over some project on the family farm. Added to this, since Sarah's death, James tends to avoid the society of young people; even that of his two nieces. I think that this is because it underlines his own loss so painfully. To have Alex with us is a rather daunting prospect and, although I long to see him, I know that James will be irritated that Vanessa has wished him upon us so casually. She and James are such different characters – he, reliable and quiet; she, casual, easy-going – and I remember how they occasionally rubbed each other up the wrong way in those early days.

I wonder how I can introduce the subject, reminding James of those happy times when we were all young together, so leading him round gently to the idea of having Alex to stay for a few weeks. After all, he is the boy's godfather.

I watch him as he sits staring into the fire. His forearms rest along his thighs, his hands are clasped loosely between his knees. The thick fair hair is not grey but it has faded and he has put on a little weight since those rugby playing days. Even then, Tony and James showed their different backgrounds despite their similarity in colouring and dress. Tony's is a bleached thin aristocratic blondness, his features are bony, his figure attenuated. He has inherited a large estate and a title to go with it. James is broad and sturdy; his hair like straw, his colour high. He comes of yeoman stock and when he rubs shoulders with the local farmers, before ascending to the auctioneer's platform, he looks like one of them. He speaks their language and they like and respect him. His elder brother and his father manage the farm so James chose to be a chartered surveyor and auctioneer.

As I watch him, he takes off his spectacles in a familiar gesture, seizing the frames between finger and thumb and holding them at arm's length, his elbow resting on his knee. At once he looks quite different: older but oddly unprotected and more vulnerable. He massages the bridge of his nose and his eyes and I feel an aching tenderness for him. I suspect that he is thinking of Sarah – do we ever recover from the pain of loss? – and I abandon all thoughts of mentioning the letter.

Now I lean forward and touch him lightly on the arm. 'Bedtime?'

He nods, smiling at me, and after the last night ritual of milk bottles and fires we climb the stairs and later, when we turn out our lights, he holds me closely, calmly, peacefully. He falls asleep quickly but I lie awake, staring into the velvety darkness, and the memories re-present themselves, smoothly unwinding behind my open eyes . . . .

I remember how difficult it was to make the transition between customer and assistant; learning to call the women 'Madam', the men 'Sir.' Very few men came to our counters. Occasionally, a brave husband would select a scarf or handkerchiefs but only at Christmas did we become besieged by last minute male shoppers, buying our boxed selections and enjoying a jolly joke or a mild flirtation in the process. I am glad that I spent that first Christmas downstairs in the haberdashery department. I can recall the seasonal excitement, the decorations going up, the faint ebb and flow of the sound of the carols being played outside the main doors – no canned music in those days – the bustle and the fun.

I joined Winslow's in the autumn and by Christmas the two Carols had unbent towards me and had taken me under their respective wings. I think that Little Carol would have been quite ready to accept me much earlier. She was a friendly girl, who really wanted to work with animals and was merely biding her time until a position should present itself in some veterinary's practice or at a riding stable. However, she was held in check by Big Carol who was of a much more cautious disposition. She held her position as senior sales assistant very seriously and, oddly, it was my usurping of this position that finally broke down the barriers between us. It happened this way. A few weeks after my arrival, having learned the stock and watched the procedure of selling, I knew that I must take my courage in my hands and approach the customers rather than waiting to be shouted for when the other girls were busy. I was very nervous; my hands sticky; my throat dry. Nevertheless I realised that, as the most junior member of the department, I should be the one to do the donkey work. Consequently, when the next customer came to the counter, I jumped forward without waiting for the Carols and said breathlessly, 'May I help you, Madam?'

Whether I could or not evades me and it is unimportant, the fact was that for a while afterwards there was a distinctly frosty atmosphere. Little Carol looked embarrassed; Big

Carol looked severe. Later, at lunch in the canteen, Little
Carol took me to task.

'You shouldn't've done that,' she said, biting into a large
cheese roll. 'Big Carol's ever so upset.'

'Done what?' I stared at her anxiously. 'What have I
done?'

'Serving that customer,' explained Little Carol, through
slowly masticating jaws. 'Pushing in like that in front
of her.'

'Pushing . . .?'

'Big Carol's senior. She gets first go.' She swallowed her
mouthful and took a refreshing pull at her glass of milk –
the tea and coffee had to be tasted to be believed – as I
gazed at her blankly.

'I thought that as I was the most junior I ought to be the
one – you know? – dashing about and things.'

She regarded me pityingly. 'It's the commission, innit?
Senior assistant has first go so as to earn the most
commission.'

'Oh God!' I said slowly. 'I didn't think of that. Oh, my
God! Well, I can give Big Carol the commission, can't I? I
didn't realise . . . .'

I was so upset that she had no difficulty in believing me
sincere and, back in the department, I hurried up to Big
Carol to explain the reason for my error. Little Carol stood
beside us, putting in a word, and Big Carol, no doubt taken
aback at the extent of my remorse, graciously forgave me.
It was then that they decided that I was not safe out alone
and drew me into their small circle of friends. I was very
grateful. My relationship with David Eastwell had made the
breaking of ice extremely difficult but now the ice began
to thaw of its own accord, the stiffness melted, and I was
accepted. It helped that Miss Tremlett so cordially disliked
me. There was absolutely no fear of favouritism here. She
harried and bullied me all the day long; sharp elbows in

my ribs; bony fingers in my back. It was unfortunate that some of the wealthy account customers were my mother's – well, my father's – friends. There were shrieks when they spotted me skulking behind a display of silk scarves.

'Oh, do look, Monica! Joan! Come over here! It's Fiona. Darling, how too funny to think of you working. Now come on, girls. We must buy something. You get commission? You do? Well then . . . .'

I would glance anxiously round for Big Carol who would grimace and jerk her head, only too pleased to let me deal with these women who had the ability to render her tongue-tied. They bought yards of elastic and ribbon they did not need, shrieking all the while at the possible use for it, and then would plunge on round the counter to buy several silk scarves and boxes of handkerchiefs. Miss Tremlett was angry when she found me serving such a bevy whilst the Carols stood idly by and it was Mrs Bateman who placidly observed that I was attracting custom which otherwise the department would not have. Meanwhile, I tried to avoid such encounters which threatened my new feelings of belonging and which caused me to suffer pangs of divided loyalties. The Carols, however, decided that it really wasn't my fault and, no doubt pitying me for knowing such appalling people, drew me more firmly into their group. I can picture them quite clearly: Enid from perfumery – maquillaged, manicured, dainty; Lorraine from leather goods – curly dark hair, turned up nose and a wide friendly grin; Margaret from hosiery – shy and sweet. Rarely could we manage to take our breaks together but several of us could be found at regular intervals in the canteen, bemoaning our lot or enjoying the latest scandal. Often my most recent idiocy would be related amidst screams of laughter. It seemed difficult for these girls – even for sweet shy Margaret – to believe that I could be so unbelievably stupid. I never felt resentful. Their mirth was so genuine, so lacking in spite; their affection for me evident.

I see us now, heads bent together, listening to Little Carol's unexpectedly deep hoarse voice . . . .

'. . . so Madam puts her two forefingers on the counter, see? Couple of feet apart. Measuring like, for her ribbon, and she says to Fiona,' (her voice takes on a haughty drawl) ' "What's that, d'you think?" And Fiona stares at her, dumb like, and Madam frowns and says, "Surely you've got some idea, girl?" and she bangs these two fingers on the counter and Fiona says, like she's had some sort of inspiration, "Two fingers?" '

I laugh with them, remembering how Little Carol had clapped her hand over her mouth and disappeared round to 'Scarves' from whence a low wailing floated out. When 'Madam' – assured finally that I was not being insolent – had made her purchase and departed, I went to find Little Carol. The sight of me sent her off into another fit of laughter and, at the memory, I chuckle aloud . . . .

James stirs, muttering in his sleep, and rolls away and I lie quite still, thinking about Vanessa again and when I first saw her.

It was my father who insisted that, now that I was earning, I should pay my share towards the housekeeping. My mother stared distressfully at my one pound note and my ten shilling note – I was earning six pounds a week – and pushed them back at me.

'I don't want it,' she said. 'Honestly, darling! What am I supposed to do with thirty shillings?'

Away she went to her studio, too wrapped up in her own creative processes to be interested in my small achievements. My father, who suffered similarly at her talented hands, had always made great efforts to see that I understood how the creative mind carried its own responsibilities. He tried hard to make certain that I knew that no personal slight was ever intended by her indifference and suggested, gently and lovingly, that we should feel honoured to be attached to such a special and gifted woman.

I carried my thirty shillings to Alma who received it sensibly. 'Come in handy that will,' she said, putting it in a jug on the dresser. 'Well done! It'll do towards Mr Jenkins' bill.' Mr Jenkins delivered the groceries. 'Very useful now you're at home full-time, eating your head off.'

It didn't occur to me that, without my school fees to pay, Mr Jenkins' bill was hardly likely to keep my father awake at night and I felt absurdly pleased with my contribution. The rest of my wage packet was mine to do with as I pleased and, since my father dropped me at Winslow's on his way to the office, my travelling expenses were light. The canteen refreshments were subsidised so I had a nice little sum to deploy. My first interest was clothes. It was Lorraine – she of the dark curly hair and warm smile – who reminded me that I would be given a discount on any item I purchased in Winslow's. So it was that I found myself in the boutique on the third floor, looking at Mary Quant look-alikes, imitation Chanel suits and miniskirts. It was Lorraine who guided me round the rails – we were all going to a cinema and on to an Indian restaurant after work – and suggested one or two outfits. Even to my untutored eye they looked quite unsuitable.

It was then that I saw Vanessa. She was sitting behind a spindly gilt table on a spindly gilt chair and looking unutterably bored. I was struck by her beauty and her elegance and, sensing my stare, she glanced up, raised her eyebrows and put both elbows on the table. It was clear that she recognised Lorraine and had no intention of putting herself out for a mere member of staff. Her long sleek bob of dark chestnut coloured hair swung forward and she stretched out her long thin legs so that her narrow feet in their low-heeled sling-backed shoes protruded from beneath the table top.

'Hi, Lorraine,' she said casually. 'There's nothing new. It's all exactly the same as it was when you looked at it yesterday. And the day before.'

Lorraine hunched a shoulder, turning her back, and pulled me with her out of the boutique. She looked quite cross – for Lorraine.

'Stuck up cow!' she said, as we climbed the stairs to the canteen. 'Thinks she's somebody, she does!'

'Who is she?' I ventured.

'Vanessa something or other. Vahnessaah!' Lorraine drawled the word in what she fondly imagined to be an upper-class accent. She drew down the corners of her mouth and half shut her eyes. 'Oh, we aren't half posh! Her dad's one of the directors.'

I was silent. People in glass houses shouldn't throw stones. Lorraine saw my face and poked me with her elbow.

'Oh, go on. She's not like you. Thinks she's better'n us, 'cos she works in the boutique, see? Wouldn't've got the job if it hadn't been for her dad.'

'Neither would I,' I said guiltily as we swung into the canteen and went up to the counter, 'if it hadn't been for mine.'

'Go on.' She gave me another nudge and addressed herself to the woman behind the counter. 'Hello Marge. What've you got to poison us with today then, love?'

The badinage flew thick and fast before we finally carried our coffee and buns to a corner table. Lorraine greeted several cronies and then gave another nod to an extremely handsome young man. I had never seen him before – I would surely have noticed him! – but her words gave me the clue.

'Hi Geoff. Had a good holiday, then?'

He answered smilingly, rather as though he was good-humouredly tolerating her, and – quite unaccountably – I felt myself blushing a little.

'That's Geoffrey Hodge,' said Lorraine, without bothering to lower her voice. 'He's a real terror, he is. Don't go listening to a word he says.' She raised her voice another decibel or two. 'I'm just warning her, Geoff, OK? Don't go trying your tricks on with her, that's all!'

I knew an exquisite embarrassment but, when I risked a look at him, he was still smiling and, catching my eye, he gave me a tiny wink accompanied by a shake of the head which made nonsense of Lorraine's accusations. Hot with all kinds of pleasurable emotions I concentrated on my coffee, wishing I was able to dress in a pretty pink bouclé wool suit – such as Vanessa had been wearing – instead of our uniform of white shirts and black skirts.

'Thank God it's nearly Christmas,' Lorraine was saying. 'We'll have a bit of fun then. How's the old Trembler then? What an old horror she is.'

'I must say it's nicest when she's off buying or at one of the other branches,' I admitted, trying not to sneak a glance at Geoffrey Hodge. 'Still, I'm going to china and glass after Christmas. They've been moving the department onto the fifth floor with furniture and soft furnishings. I'll miss the Carols, though.'

'You're never!' Lorraine was gazing at me with such undisguised horror that I felt alarmed.

'Never what?'

'Never going to china and glass? Not to old Frozen Face Ferrars? Christ! She's a hundred times worse than old Trembler!'

I stared back at her, Geoffrey Hodge forgotten. 'How do you mean? Who did you say?'

'Mrs God Almighty Ferrars. Looks like she's swallowed a poker.' She shook her head. 'You won't last two minutes up there. Like a bloody mausoleum, it is. All that furniture and ever so quiet. Everyone's at least fifty up there. Like an old people's home. Well, Brenda Grice is OK. She's soft furnishings. She's a bit of a laugh but honestly, Fiona, you don't want to go up there.'

'It's been arranged,' I said feebly. 'I'm going to be trained as a buyer.'

'Go on!' She grinned at me. 'You can't sell half a yard of elastic without some sort of disaster.'

'I know.' I grinned back. 'But I'm going to have to give it a go. My father's offered me a car if I can stick at it.'

'Phew!' She opened her eyes at me. 'A car, eh! All right for some. Well, I suppose it'll be worth it for a car.'

She sounded frankly sceptical and I was relieved when Geoffrey Hodge paused by the table on his way out thus distracting her attention. He also distracted mine.

'I s'pose you want to know who she is,' said Lorraine, without preamble. 'Her name's Fiona Marchant. And watch it! Her dad's a pal of the Old Man, see?'

'How do you do?'

He held out his hand and I shook it, feeling a fool and at a disadvantage sitting down.

'I'm Geoffrey Hodge,' he said. 'I'm head of the travel goods department.'

'She's on haberdashery,' said Lorraine, as though I was unable to speak for myself. 'So if you come sneaking round you'll get an earful from old Trembler!'

He laughed. 'I hope you don't believe everything Lorraine tells you,' he said. 'I'm quite harmless really.'

I mumbled something banal and watched him go out.

'Good looking sod, he is,' said Lorraine reflectively, her eyes on my flushed face. 'Just watch him, that's all!'

*   *   *

I turn restlessly in bed, pulling the quilt about my shoulders. James breathes deeply and regularly beside me and I snuggle closer to his warmth, relaxing and stretching, and presently I, too, sleep.

3

James has left for the office and still I have not told him of Alex's impending visit. I woke from a vivid happy dream. We had been young again, in my dream; Vanessa and Tony; James and I. We were having one of those ridiculously delightful picnics which were to become our 'thing'. By the middle sixties it was necessary, somehow, to be breaking away, bending the rules, and this was our – very mild! – gesture of defiance; Vanessa's and mine that is, not the boys'. They were on holiday from the agricultural college. It was Vanessa and I who sneaked out from Winslow's at lunchtimes to be whirled away on these expeditions. Cold roast chicken and strawberries in a wicker hamper; a bottle of champagne and delicious bitter coffee from a flask. Vanessa and I would sit on the thick soft rug whilst Tony organised the food and James dealt with the bottle, the champagne frothing into wide-mouthed, shallow crystal. We'd tune the radio car to some pirate station, listening to the Beatles or some other group, Vanessa leaping up to jig around until Tony would seize her and dance with her or they would fall, laughing, to the ground together. Afterwards the three of us smoked cigarettes whilst James, stretched out on the grass, would draw on his pipe . . . .

I rouse slowly, reluctantly, still half held within my dream, and turn to press closer to James – not the young handsome

relaxed man of my dream but still my beloved James –
putting my arm round his inert form. He stirs, groaning,
and wakes, twisting to glance at his watch.

'Christ! It's nearly eight o'clock!'

He flings back the quilt and swings his feet to the floor,
rumpling his hair, whilst I lay back on my pillow feeling
absurdly put out. It is quite foolish to expect him to share
my mood; nevertheless I feel as if I have been rebuffed.
I make no effort to rise with him but stay, head averted,
pretending to be still half asleep. He pauses by my side of
the bed.

'Are you OK?'

'Mm.' I keep my eyes closed, testing the quality of the
silence between us. It is not a sympathetic silence. There
will be no quick kiss, no 'well, you stay there and I'll bring
you a cup of coffee.' The silence is edging on the resentful. I
know he is late, that he has an early meeting about which he
is worried, yet I cling to my feeling of unreasonable hurt.

Now, an hour or so later, I eat my breakfast and brood
upon the delicate mechanism that exists in an intimate,
on-going relationship between a man and a woman. I see
this relationship as a long intricate dance; sometimes the
dance becomes almost tribal, aggressive, with stamping feet,
waving fists and ugly contorted mouths. At other times each
rests peacefully against the other, smiling dreamily, the
rhythm slows and our arms go out to encircle the loved one,
drawing close, heart against heart, eyes closed. Most of the
time, however, the steps are weaving, dexterous, advancing,
giving ground, circling, hesitating, marking time. We watch
our partner's movements, studying the body language; the
energy or lassitude of movement; summing up, giving out,
rejecting, in turn.

As I crunch away at my toast, which is loaded with
my own home-made marmalade, and pour a second cup
of coffee, I try to decide at which point the need for

subterfuge, emotional blackmail, the cut and thrust, enters these relationships. Do we even recognise that we are using these stratagems? Surely we do. These little parrying lunges on the matrimonial dance floor are so integral with the daily round. I think of my earlier passage with James . . . .

I continue to lie still, hearing him washing, shaving, dressing, and I know that I should be downstairs, making the coffee – James does not eat breakfast – and being at hand lest there should be some last minute drama or to boost his confidence regarding this meeting. My guilt increases so that, when he appears with my coffee, I am ready to smile at him, receive it gratefully and then gulp it back so as to hurry down to be with him.

He ignores my smile – which I can feel is both placatory and slightly anxious – puts the coffee down with a sharp click and straightens with a grimace, hand to the small of the back. His eyes carefully avoid mine but his expression is pained. He is suffering, irritable, wishing to increase my guilt which correspondingly diminishes. My smile fades. Aha! I recognise this sequence of the dance and take my own preparatory steps.

'Thanks,' I say abruptly, hauling myself up and frowning slightly. 'I had a terrible night. My head's bursting.'

James hesitates, his movements are less assured, he falters. My mother died of a brain haemorrhage; dropping down – now here, now gone – after a series of appallingly agonising headaches. I, too, have headaches and I know that James fears them.

'Do . . . do you want me to get your tablets?' he asks but with a touch of impatience.

His steps are still too quick for my slower pace. They tap about, prepared to slow a little, but indicating that mine must hurry along to catch up so as to synchronise with his.

'No thanks.' I cannot bring myself to dance to his tune,

even if it is now a slower, gentler tune. 'I'll be OK if I can just relax.'

He pauses, shrugs and goes away and as I sip my coffee – now dust and ashes in my mouth – I wonder how it is possible for us to get so far out of step with each other. Why should a couple who can whirl and glide and sway so happily together be able quite unexpectedly to trip and stumble, step on each other's toes? The well-known movements, the smooth meshing of pace, the harmony, have vanished and all at once we find that we are clasping a stranger in our arms; a stranger with unfriendly eyes and a sullen, petulant mouth. Back we start from this alien! We are fearful and cross. We have been deceived, lulled by pretty tunes, seductive chords. We weave and stamp, eyeing each other across the dance floor, watchful and wary. Sometimes suddenly, sometimes more slowly, the tempo changes again and a twist or a turn shows us our beloved, familiar and reassuring, and we stretch out our arms, tentatively trying out the well-tried steps which sweep us back into the dance.

In our fear of neglect or of losing love we react in self-defence. Our affection is the bargaining counter; now withheld, now generously offered. I am reminded of Christ's words at the Last Supper. 'A new commandment I give unto you, That ye love one another.' Yes, well. It sounds so simple and is, in reality, so difficult to sustain. I finish my breakfast feeling ashamed. The telephone rings and it is James.

'I just wondered,' gruffly, 'if your head's any better?'

'Oh, darling,' I say swiftly. 'Oh how sweet of you to phone. Yes it is. Much better. How did the meeting go?'

'Oh, not too bad at all . . . Better get on, then. See you tonight.'

'Yes. Yes, of course. I love you, James.'

'Mm.' Someone is with him but his voice holds a brief warm, intimate note. 'Me too. Bye.'

I feel light, happy, relieved, thankful. We are back in the dance!

The first time Geoffrey Hodge took me out we went to a disco. As I wash up my breakfast things I try to remember how that first date came about. It eludes me. Certainly there was a great deal of cautious manoeuvring at the beginning. He had a reputation within Winslow's which worried me and embarrassed him. Slow and stupid as I was, even I noticed that he would appear at unexpected moments; coming down the stairs pretending to look for a colleague; dashing into the canteen for a hasty cup of coffee at my early hour; lingering outside the staff entrance when it was time to go home. It did not occur to me that these were the first steps of a courtship ritual, however, until the two Carols and Lorraine took it upon themselves to open my eyes. I began to dread their nudges and grimaces, the winks and grins. I burned with shame lest he should think that I encouraged them.

The two Carols were models of subtlety compared with Lorraine. Her piercing remarks and forthright observations exposed and defeated Geoffrey's would-be-casual approach and at last – I discovered this much later – he very cleverly took her into his confidence. From that moment she began to promote his cause. I was very happy to be persuaded, despite – perhaps because of – his reputation. After all, there was no real harm. He liked pretty girls but tired of them quickly and abandoned them promptly. It was, apparently, a case of a few dates and a few kisses and then a new pretty girl would appear on his horizon and he would be off, unable to resist this latest attraction. There were one or two sore hearts scattered about the store and several girls who worshipped him from afar but I did not wish to be of their number. I decided that this time I would be the one to call the shots; keeping the whole thing light, casual and simply fun.

Where and when Geoffrey finally made the invitation I cannot recall but I *do* remember mentioning it to Lorraine whilst loitering in the leather goods department on my way back from my lunch. Mrs Cotton – the head of the department and a thoroughly delightful lady – was listening in. She beamed at us.

'Going out with Geoffrey, dear?' She nodded approvingly. 'That's right. He takes out all the pretty girls in turn.'

'Mrs Cotton!' cried Lorraine, scandalised. 'It isn't like that. He . . . he feels different this time.' She glanced at me quickly, anxiously. 'Fiona's special. He's really crazy about her.'

I was almost as embarrassed by Lorraine's unexpected descent from cynicism to unashamed romanticism as I was about my affairs being discussed so publicly. I mumbled inarticulately whilst Mrs Cotton smiled pityingly and disbelievingly.

'That's nice then,' she said soothingly. 'Have a good time, love.'

I had a wonderful time. I had never been to a disco before and the kaleidoscope of light and noise – as well as the wine – disorientated and enchanted me. By the third dance I had forgotten all about being light and casual. Smooching to the Beatles' – 'Yesterday' I think it was – I was already too much in love to be anything of the kind. Nevertheless, my shyness and my absolute lack of experience helped me to keep a formality between us which helped to disguise my feelings.

Had I realised it, this was my trump card. Geoffrey Hodge was a cut above most of the shop assistants in Winslow's and he was used to easy conquests and to calling the tune. Most of the girls were in awe of him; flattered by his attention, secretly overawed by his sophisticated approach. When he took me home in his father's car it was his turn to be overawed. I remember that he called my father 'Sir' – my mother had long since gone to bed – and was reluctant to answer his fairly searching questions. The mood – created by the disco and those deliciously intimate moments of the drive home afterwards – was broken. I remember my hot, fidgety embarrassment which took the form of offhandedness and I know that when I encountered Geoffrey on the following Monday morning I was prepared for a coolness to have sprung up between us. I wondered whether he might have joked about my father to some of the girls. Some older wiser woman inhabited my skin that morning, driving out the young love-sick eager girl and presenting a brittle exterior.

I had, however, quite misread the situation. Geoffrey was a social climber and a snob but more importantly he was one of those people that, having made a conquest, immediately lost interest. He was deceived by the brittle formality which hid my true feelings and he had been impressed by my home and my father. Naturally I did not realise this at the time. I was much too relieved to see him – hurrying past my counter on some pretence; giving me a warm special smile; in the canteen at my early lunch hour – to analyse the situation. I advanced with a caution which was guaranteed to hold his interest. He used Lorraine subtly, as a go-between. Between the leather goods department and the luggage department there was always a certain amount of communication and now, when I met Lorraine in the canteen, she had a mouthful of his compliments ready for me.

I listened readily but hid my reaction. Young and inexperienced I might be but I had heard too many secrets spilled at these tables to believe that my own might be sacrosanct. Let Geoffrey bare his soul to Lorraine if he chose, my feelings would remain opaque, masked from her eager glances by an unruffled expression. She was faintly puzzled by this; urging his suit, singing his praises. I was puzzled, too. It seemed so unlike the cynical caustic Lorraine. It hadn't occurred to me that running not too far beneath that worldly-wise surface was a rich vein of romanticism. More than that; Lorraine was not too far from being in love with him herself. Geoffrey was the type whose nature it was to captivate every woman within his orbit. Even dear motherly Mrs Cotton with her rinsed blue hair and exotically winged spectacles must not be immune from his charm. She adored him. Between them they wooed me for him.

I see this now from the vantage of middle age. Then, I was merely aware of the heightening of the tension; excited by the sidelong glances and unexpected meetings. When he was certain of my answer, he invited me to the theatre. There was great excitement about this. I learned that none of my little group had ever been to the theatre and the relationship was invested with even more glamour. It was Shaw's *Major Barbara*. Lorraine wrinkled her nose, baffled that we should wish to waste an evening thus when we could be snogging in the back row of the stalls in some cinema, but she liked the sophistication of it.

Alone this time, I visited the boutique on the third floor. Vanessa glanced at me as I sidled along the racks of clothes. She was unpacking a box of garments but she stood up and wandered towards me.

'Hello,' she said easily. 'I've seen you before, haven't I?'

I nodded, remembering what Lorraine had told me and feeling a little shy. 'I'm on haberdashery,' I said.

She sighed. It was a companionable sigh; a 'whatever are we doing here?' kind of sigh which included me in the ludicrousness of our situation.

'Honestly,' she said, giving a disdainful little shrug, 'isn't it too dreary for words? Have you been bullied into it, too?'

I looked at her, surprised at her perspicacity. 'Well, actually . . . Yes. I couldn't think of anything I wanted to do.'

She nodded. 'Me too. Listen. Why don't we go and have some lunch?'

'I've had my lunch,' I explained 'I go at twelve.'

'At *twelve*?'

'I know.' I shrugged and then frowned. 'I've never seen you in the canteen.'

'I don't go to the canteen, darling.' She looked quite horrified. 'I go out.'

'*Out*?' I gaped at her.

She grinned. 'Down the back stairs and a quick dash for freedom. You should try it. So what are you looking for?'

I told her about my trip to the theatre and mentioned Geoffrey. She gave another little shrug. It was just as disdainful as the first one and I felt awkward; as though she were criticising me.

'He's very good-looking, of course.' The observation seemed to excuse my rather questionable taste. 'You must come out with me one evening and meet my gang.'

It sounded tempting and I said that I should love to, quite boldly. She drifted along the rack until she found a black mini-dress. It was restrained and sexy all at the same time and quite unlike the garments Lorraine would have chosen for me.

'Try it,' she said, tossing it into my arms.

It was perfect. The price tag made me gulp a little but Vanessa was firm.

'Look upon it as an investment,' she advised. 'It's a classic of its kind. You'll wear it and wear it. You can pay in instalments but don't tell anyone.'

She was right about my wearing it and wearing it. How I loved that dress! Geoff's expression when he saw me in it made it worth every penny. Over the following months Vanessa guided my taste in clothes so that I built up a very exciting wardrobe but it wasn't until I moved up to china and glass that we really became friends.

*   *   *

As I put away the breakfast things and begin the usual round of chores, I think about her letter again and decide, reluctantly, that I should tell James about it this evening. After all, why should I hesitate? Is it because I know that he is tired and worried; his mood uncertain? Or is it because I came to dread the annoyance with which he finally regarded Vanessa when she left Tony, taking the small Alex with her to France, there to embark on a series of affairs. James's sympathy was all for Tony. She *was* very naughty, of course, but after the sombre atmosphere of the fifth floor, her light-hearted approach was a very attractive one to me and I forgave her everything simply because she made me laugh and lent my life colour and excitement. Through her I met James . . . .

I recall the false steps we made earlier this morning and determine that we shall have a happy evening together. I shall cook his favourite dinner and, if necessary, the letter must be postponed for one more day.

4

As I finish my household tasks and write up my notes taken at the last Parochial Church Council meeting – I am the secretary – I brood over the dinner I shall cook for James. When Sarah died I took to good works. Perhaps, if I had been qualified, I might have found myself a job – in an office or teaching. As it was I seized on anything which might fill the long hours and distract my mind from my grief. How empty and quiet the house was! I used to roam about; going into rooms, staring out of windows, making endless cups of coffee. James went to the office earlier each morning and returned later each evening, often stopping to snatch a bite at the pub on the way home. It was a joint decision that we should move out of the sprawling Edwardian villa which no longer echoed with childish voices, whose rooms were bare of discarded toys, whose garden lay peaceful and unused; the swing hanging idly, emptily, from the old apple tree. The memories were too painful.

The move gave us employment which occupied our spare hours and an endless topic of conversation to fill the terrible silences which fell between us. The village was only twenty minutes away from the quiet tree-lined street where we had lived for nearly fifteen years, so we were still within easy reach of James's office and our friends and family. My father

– to my great surprise – married again; a young, managing, cheerful woman whom I dislike intensely. When he had a slight stroke I was grateful for her practical ability to care for him. I visit regularly and she and I hide our antagonism behind pleasant smiles. This is a different type of dance. We advance and retreat, maintaining a formality at all times, and only rarely step on each other's toes.

The dance, of course, is not confined to married couples or like partnerships. Our own children join in; first rocked gently in our arms, then jogged upon our shoulders until they take their own first tentative steps. They skip and hop and we slow the rhythm, holding their hands lest they fall. Soon their paces stretch to match our own but, all too soon, they outstrip us, whirling away to their own music, fingers clicking, inventing different sequences, finding new partners. Sarah made her exit early from the dance and James and I were obliged to retrace our old steps, seeking forgotten routines.

I cannot now remember when I first became aware of a reservation in James. It seems to have been there from the beginning but, when Sarah died, it took on a new depth. Perhaps it was because we feared we might never have a child – and because we were never successful again after her birth – that she became so precious to us. Our grief is fathomless. Secretly we have observed other children over the years, thinking, 'Sarah would have been that age now'; 'would have been going to university'; 'would be bringing boyfriends home'; but we do not share these thoughts. I know, instinctively, that James simply could not bear it just as I know when he is thinking about her. It is strange how he comforts me but refuses to be comforted. He appears to grieve on two levels. Up to a point we are able to share our sorrow but, beyond that point, I am gently but intransigently closed out. Was that reserve there when I first met him?

Whilst I prepare the dinner – peeling, cutting, shredding – I slip back again into the past.

My removal to the fifth floor was regarded with a kind of sympathetic gloom. I felt as if I were going on some dangerous but necessary expedition from which I might never return. So nervous did I become that, one teatime, I slipped up to the fifth floor and had a look for myself. The vast spaces, filled with furniture, were silent and oppressive after the bustle of the ground floor. A few salesmen paced the aisles. In their dark suits they looked forbidding and I avoided them. The china and glass department was tucked away in one corner, separated from the soft furnishing department by the bedding department. Unobserved, I slunk to the entrance and peered in, noting the shelves of figurines and dinner services and the sparkling crystal, but my attention was all for the woman who sat behind her glass-fronted desk at the back of the department. Her dark head was bent over her paperwork and she seemed quite isolated, incarcerated by that tall glass wall which enclosed her on three sides. Beside it was a small desk, at present unoccupied.

Already I had heard the gossip. Brenda Grice wanted to run this department but Elizabeth Ferrars, having already reached the position of buyer in another store, had been given the position over Brenda Grice's head. Everyone said that it was a shame; that Brenda Grice was good fun and would have been much better than Elizabeth Ferrars who was a cold fish . . . .

She raised her head, staring down the length of the department, and I fled away, frowned upon by the two furniture salesmen.

I was so nervous by this time that I almost thought of going to the personnel manager and asking if I might be allowed to stay where I was. It was Geoffrey who dissuaded me. The china and glass department had class and I was to be trained properly. He couldn't understand why I should want to remain on the haberdashery counter like Little Carol; unremarked and unambitious.

By this time I was quite infatuated with him. Luckily – and it *was* luck and not judgment – I was still unable to show it and so I was still interesting to him. The evening at the theatre had been a success but we were not yet at ease with one another. We could not have wandered through the streets together, stopping off at a coffee bar or drifting aimlessly into a cinema, as did other young couples. Our meetings still required formal arrangements. I vividly remember the shock and the passion I felt when he first kissed me. It was at a party – but whose? Some friend of his, I think, who was leaving the town was giving a farewell party. Because the guests were all young like ourselves, and mainly couples, it was the most relaxed evening we had yet spent together. These others looked upon us as a long-standing couple, treated us as such, and it was rather exciting to accept their evaluation. Geoffrey became more demonstrative and rather possessive; chatting to his friends with his arm draped negligently about my shoulder; deciding on which wine I would prefer to drink. I loved it. When a record was put on and couples began to dance I slipped happily into his arms. The music was slow and we smooched, just like everyone else, until we reached a darker, quieter corner.

I had enjoyed a brief holiday romance with a schoolfriend's brother – an innocent, brief affair which had included several extremely amateur attempts at kissing. Just *how* amateur I discovered when Geoffrey kissed me in that dark corner. I think I learned quickly. No doubt Miss Tremblett would have been surprised at my aptitude. My luck held. It was I – confused, overwhelmed, frightened, even – who drew back first. I felt weak and my knees shook but I still had enough self-control to stop while I was able. Geoffrey's reluctance gave me a sense of power which was quite delightful and I was able to remain firm. This, had I but realised it, gave me a stay of execution and the relationship moved into the next stage.

I see now that Geoffrey and I were ill-matched for the dance. His steps were smooth, polished, dexterous; selected for their showmanship. They were executed with panache and with calculated charm. I was too slow, too cautious for him. I stumbled, breaking the rhythm, and, before too long, my hesitations began to irritate a little, spoiling the dramatic effect of his own performance. This display of ill-humour first made itself felt one lunchtime. I suspect that Geoffrey needed to see my capitulation; my helpless adoration. This had happened in his previous romantic whirlings and he saw no reason why the pattern should not continue. My continued resistance was beginning to irk him. Naturally I did not analyse it so at the time. I was certainly bewitched enough to feel anxiety at his irritation. Encouraged by my behaviour at the party, and on one or two following occasions, he had gone so far as to book – without checking with me – two tickets for the ballet; the Bolshoi.

As I roll out pastry in my warm comfortable kitchen, I try to remember why I could not go. It must have been something important for me to refuse his invitation. As I wipe my floury hands and fetch a dish, I see his face quite clearly, superimposed against my cork notice board, and, clasping the pie dish to my bosom, I am transported back in time to the staff canteen; the smells, the chatter, the sense of familiarity . . . .

My heart beat fast in dismay as I took in his petulant look; the lowering of his eyelids with their long dark lashes, the droop of the sensuous mouth. His skin had an odd pallor which accentuated the dark hazel of his eyes and the blackness of his hair.

'I'm sorry,' I faltered – *why* did I refuse? – 'but I simply can't. If only you'd mentioned it before . . . .'

My diffident criticism faltered beneath his sulky stare.

'I wanted it to be a surprise,' he said, thus increasing my guilt.

'Well . . .' I hesitated, terrified that he might suggest that he invite another girl in my place.

'I'll take them back,' he said crossly. 'They were damned expensive! Maybe I'll be able to get my money back.'

That he should display such parsimony to me came as a shock. The suave lover had vanished and, in his place, was a bad-tempered young man puffing discontentedly on his cigarette. He saw my surprise and guessed that he'd taken a step too far and that a discordant note was echoing between us. Quickly he retreated, side-stepping, weaving, intricately regaining lost ground.

'I'm sorry,' I said again – but he leaned across the table and took my hand, disregarding the interested glances of the other members of staff. He was usually very discreet.

'What must you be thinking of me?' It was a rhetorical question; even under these circumstances he was very confident. 'I'm just so bitterly disappointed. As soon as you mentioned it – you remember? A few weeks ago when we saw the poster? – I was determined to get tickets. I wanted to surprise you.'

'Oh, I know . . . .'

'And you must forgive me for mentioning the money but . . .' a humorous but resigned shrug.

He managed to imply that, on his salary, I was a rather expensive luxury and guilt bit even deeper.

'Oh, Geoff . . .' I was bitterly disappointed, too, searching for a way of making amends.

'Never mind.' He saw my guilt and disappointment and was quick to capitalise on them. 'How about staying in town this evening and we'll go to the cinema? Have a bite to eat somewhere first?'

This was the first informal invitation I had ever received from him and I knew that I must accept or risk upsetting him further.

'That would be fun,' I said quickly. 'I'll phone home and tell them. Shall . . . I'll be able to get back OK, I suppose?'

'We'll sort something out,' he said almost indifferently; and, once again, this casual approach was new to our relationship. 'Warn them that you might be late. Your father doesn't have to wait up!'

This was a definite dig at my father's old-fashioned ways but I was determined to go along with Geoff, to match my steps to his if I could. He stubbed out his cigarette, glanced at his watch, made a face and stood up.

'See you outside later, then,' he said and hurried away.

I sat on for a moment, feeling that something momentous had happened. I felt excited and alarmed all at once, wondering if I were capable of the complicated measures that lay ahead. At least I could leave a message with Alma; she might question but could not forbid. My father would have wanted to know the exact arrangements for getting me home. On my way down the back stairs I met Vanessa.

'Hi!' She was tying an emerald silk scarf over her chestnut hair. She crossed it under her chin and tied it at the back – à la Bardot – succeeding in looking glamorous and exciting. 'Just off to lunch. Sports car, darling.' She patted the scarf. 'Madly anti-hair! Now don't forget we're going to get together soon. Must dash!'

The heels of her slingbacks clattered on the uncarpeted stairs and I watched her descent, breathing in the fugitive fragrance of her expensive scent and envying her sophistication. Vanessa would consider it neither unusual nor unsettling to be invited casually to the cinema without any previous arrangements. Even by the stricter standards of those days I knew that I was old-fashioned and provincial but my father could be formidable and my mother – when she was made aware of any transgressions – was capable of an icy disgust which chilled and shamed me.

I lingered by the leather goods counter, hoping that Lorraine and Mrs Cotton would dispel that premonitory icy breath. I told them all about the tickets for the ballet and the plans for the evening. They were sympathetic, encouraging, even envious. I slipped back into my own department feeling much better. An excitement possessed me; I saw myself with Geoff in some intimate little café and imagined sitting next to him in the warm darkness of the cinema. It grieved me that I should have to go out in my dreary black and white and I contemplated a dash to the boutique during my tea break. Caution laid a cold hand on my heated imagination. My small quarterly allowance was nearly spent and Vanessa had already been more than flexible regarding my account with the boutique.

Geoffrey was waiting for me outside the staff entrance. There was a subtle shift in his attitude; accepting the jokes of our colleagues without embarrassment; taking my hand with a proprietorial ease. I noticed the glances of several of the older members of staff and felt a twinge of uneasiness. They looked at Geoff with a wariness, almost with a dislike, which worried me. It was as if I ought to feel ashamed to be with him, instead of recklessly happy and proud. The feeling persisted, joining with my anxieties as to how I should get home later. The one bus that passed through the village left the city at half past ten. By now, I knew that it made the hope of seeing the end of a theatre or film almost impossible.

Geoffrey was evidently aware that all was not well. He steered us in the direction of a very grand tea shop – it was far too early for dinner – and settled us in a secluded corner. I need not, after all, have worried about my clothes.

He helped me off with my coat, took one look at my face and, very cleverly, reverted to the subject of the tickets. It was a nice blend of disappointment, reproach and an anxiety about the waste of money that brought my own regret and guilt flying back. He manoeuvred me through the obstacles of my uneasiness with practised expertise until we were once again in step. True, he had slowed his steps a little so that I might catch up but I caught a hint of impatience that frightened me into abandoning my caution.

As I drank my tea and ate my Welsh rarebit, I was aware of his good looks. I saw other women glancing at him and the waitress, hovering, giggling at his pleasantries. The complacence in his lowered eyes I mistook for modesty and I wanted to believe that Lorraine was right and that, this time, it was different for him. I touched his hand shyly and he looked up quickly with a hastily concealed flash of triumph which puzzled me.

We were rather early at the cinema and he asked me if I minded seeing the end of the big feature. I pointed out that, if I were to catch the last bus, it might be a good idea since we might have to leave before the film ended. He was silent for a moment and then asked if there was no friend in town with whom I might stay. I said 'no' to that and the sulky look returned for a moment. I deduced from this that he was not able to have his father's car and wondered if he felt humiliated that he had no transport. I knew that he lived at home, although I had not visited it, and guessed that he could not afford to buy and run a car on his salary. Although, in those days, it was not usual for young men to have their own cars I felt a stab of sympathy for his frustrated independence and smiled at him. I wanted him to be happy and, later, when he put his arm round me I did not resist but sat close to him, disregarding the people in the row behind us. . . .

*   *   *

As I grease the pie dish and line it with pastry I feel a kind of resigned indignation at the foolish girl that I was. I remember the vulnerability, the fear of losing the beloved, the sacrifices of pride. Oh, how difficult and fraught with danger are the early steps to maturity! I shut the oven door and pour myself a large drink. Deliberately, I turn away from the past and bring my mind to bear on James and the evening ahead.

5

So immersed have I become in my recollections that, when James arrives home, I am almost surprised that he is not the young man I met all those years ago. Geoffrey's dark pale urban elegance fades – as it did then – beside the ruddy fairness of James's outdoor mien. He looks his best in tweeds and corduroys and, as he comes into the kitchen carrying a bunch of sweet-smelling jonquils and pale delicate daffodils, my heart seems to dissolve with love for him. I take the flowers and kiss his cold cheek, wondering how I could have behaved as I did earlier this morning. He, I suspect, is feeling the same. James is not your natural flowers and chocolates man.

'How lovely!' I inhale the scent luxuriously. How wonderful spring flowers are at the end of the long dark winter! It is early still for such blooms and they must have been expensive. 'They're beautiful.'

James looks pleased but nonchalant. He does not wish too much to be made of his offering. I busy myself with a vase whilst he pours us both a drink. I feel buoyed up with an expectant happiness. Neither of us is happy if our steps do not synchronise or our emotions are not in tune and, though neither of us will mention it, we are relieved that harmony has replaced the discordance of our morning exchange. Perhaps because there are no children to distract from or to dilute the tensions of our relationship, the cracks show up clearly and cannot be disguised by – or ignored in – the hurly-burly of busy family life.

At the beginning I think James feared that it was his fault that we could not make a baby. I so longed for children that he became quite desperate when none appeared and his anxiety, coupled with my own fear that I was barren, caused us many anguished hours. It added insult to injury that Vanessa became pregnant even before she and Tony were engaged. James was surprisingly prudish about it and extremely reluctant to be the baby's godfather, pointing out that his friendship with Tony was hardly on that level. I thought that he was taking it all far too seriously and told him so.

When I failed to conceive, James found it even more difficult to respond to his godson and I was relieved when Tony's father died and he assumed the running of the estate and we saw less of each other. I think it was because he feared that it made me unhappy to see the infant Alex that James became so protective towards me and I was touched. Vanessa was a casual, easy-going mother and it was difficult not to feel resentment. Once Sarah arrived all was changed but, with her death, I felt that for James the resentment returned. Why should Vanessa's child survive whilst ours should die?

Tonight, however, James is not brooding over Sarah's untimely death. He is cheerful, loving, amusing. He talks about his day and I tell him about mine and all around us is the warm glow of happiness. We have a second drink and our hands touch and cling for a moment and we both know, secretly, that we will make love tonight. The dance is sweeping us away and, as the evening advances, our gestures become slower, more languorous; our movements are leading us gently, dreamily to a necessary fulfilment.

Once or twice I think of the letter but the tender, happy

look on James's face prevents me from mentioning it. I fear to shatter this precious, fragile mood and, once again, the moment passes.

We awake from our night of love with a deliciously relaxed tenderness and, this morning, I make the coffee and bring it back upstairs so that we sit in bed, leaning together, contented, unspeaking. As I sip, I debate with myself as to whether now is the moment for me to break the news about Alex's impending visit. I try a few phrases in my head.

'Oh, by the way, I nearly forgot,' a careless approach. 'I've had a letter from Vanessa . . .'

Or perhaps I should try to involve him. 'Poor old Alex. He does so long to come back to England . . . .'

Would enthusiasm convince him? 'Lovely news, darling! Guess who's coming to stay . . .?'

'Philip phoned me yesterday,' James speaks whilst I am still trying out my lines. 'Dad's taken a turn for the worse. This wrangle with Phil over subsidies has taken it out of him a bit. I'm taking a couple of days off and going down. He wants to get a few things sorted out.'

'Oh James, I'm so sorry.' His father is very elderly and has remained on the farm with James's older brother and his wife. It has not always been a happy arrangement; wills have clashed – as has been the case recently – and James is called in to mediate and soothe. 'Is it . . .? Is he. . .?

'Oh, he'll live a bit longer yet.' James finishes his coffee and sets the mug down on the bedside table. 'But we want to get things tied up legally. I don't know how you are for committees and things but you know they'd all love to see you.'

I nod thoughtfully. 'When did you say?'

'I thought I'd travel down on Wednesday. I can stay on over the weekend if it's necessary. Philip's arranging a meeting with Mr Tompkins. We don't want any legal loopholes.'

I nod again but my mind is busy. Alex is due to arrive on Wednesday. Perhaps I need not mention the letter at all.

'I'll check my diary,' I say with a certain amount of guile and James smiles, kisses me and slides out of bed.

I sit against my pillows and watch the clouds tumbling and rolling across the sky above the church tower. The rooks rise in a flurry and once again I think of Elizabeth Ferrars, experiencing the familiar stab of guilt and shame. Did I move up to the fifth floor before Ursula Ellis arrived to tempt Geoffrey away from me? I think not. Her arrival caused rather a stir. I can recall her quite clearly; a statuesque young woman with a quantity of curling brown hair. She was a trained beautician – Elizabeth Arden? Estée Lauder? – and, along with her make-up, she wore a faintly supercilious expression. Enid, very put out, told us all about her during the coffee break. Newly arrived from London, she apparently regarded us as provincial and old-fashioned. She'd demanded certain privileges which were denied to the other girls and Enid was as cross as her excessive gentility would allow. She drew in her chin and pursed her mouth disapprovingly, patting at her rigidly coiffured hair.

'Can't see why anyone wants to eat in the restaurant anyway,' said the irrepressible Lorraine. 'There's old Tremblett sitting up straight like she's swallowed a poker, with her little finger stuck out when she drinks. And old Desperate Dan' (our soubriquet for Mr Daniels from Menswear) 'looking like he's had a swig at the vinegar bottle. Who needs it? I'd rather drink the poison old Marge dishes up in this hole!'

'That's not the point, Lorraine.' Enid blinked her mascara'd lashes rapidly, registering her annoyance with Lorraine's lack of sensibility. 'The point is, she's been set up over us and she knows it. It's not fair to the rest of us.'

'Have you had it out with Mr Kerr?' growled Little Carol.

Enid made a face which adequately conveyed contempt without actually being vulgar. We all nodded understandingly. Mr Kerr always took the easy option.

Lorraine shrugged. 'So she walks in and out through the front door and eats with the miseries in the restaurant. So who cares? And anyway, if she's that wonderful, what's she doing here? Why isn't she still in London?'

For a moment Enid forgot herself for long enough to look almost animated. Instinctively we all bent towards her. 'There are rumours that she got the push from Peter Jones,' she said in a hushed voice. We exchanged glances and then collectively jumped as Big Carol's voice hissed furiously above our heads.

'D'you two know what the time is? Miss Tremblett's having fits. She's sent me up to fetch you. For God's sake get a move on. . . .'

'Still dreaming?' James's voice breaks in on my thoughts. 'Well, why not? Have a bit of a quiet morning. Would you like some more coffee?'

I smile at him and, because I know that he wants to make this gesture, I agree to another cup of coffee. How different this is from yesterday! I stretch luxuriously and, when James has brought the coffee and kissed me goodbye, I let my thoughts drift back to Ursula Ellis. . . .

I did not fear her at first. I was still quite besotted by Geoffrey but now I was beginning to let it show. Why not? I had begun to believe that I *was* different from those others and, as the spring evenings lengthened, we had taken to strolling in the city parks and going to the zoo on Sunday afternoons. Subtly his attitude continued to change. He took the kisses as his right, now, and once, when he attempted a too intimate embrace from which I quite instinctively shrank, I saw the sulky look again.

'For heaven's sake!' he muttered impatiently and turned from me to light a cigarette.

I was frightened by his reaction. It was not an era when sex was discussed freely and I knew only what I had gleaned from the girls at school and from what Alma had intimated. She had talked darkly about 'going too far' and 'keeping a man's respect'. Things were a little different when the engagement ring was bought but, until then, a girl allowed no liberties to be taken. I had only a hazy idea as to what 'liberties' might be but – naively – I had not imagined that Geoffrey would take them. His impatience implied that he expected me to go along with his love-making and I was confused and miserable as I sat on the bench in a quiet part of the park on that early summer evening. He had his back half turned to me and I heard him sigh heavily.

'I suppose you think I should apologise?' he asked with a kind of amused irritation.

I felt immature and foolish. His tone implied that I was and I did not know how to reply. He sighed again and I remember thinking that, unless I was more obliging, I might lose him.

'You took me by surprise,' I explained defensively but with a conciliatory note.

'Having your breast touched isn't the end of the world,' he said contemptuously and I recoiled a little at the brutality in his voice.

Just as he had over the business of the tickets, so now he sensed that he had nearly gone too far. He threw away his half smoked cigarette and turned to look at me. The sulky look was replaced by a familiar one of humorous resignation and he reached for my hand.

'You can't blame me if I get carried away,' he murmured. 'I'm not made of asbestos, you know.'

I was so relieved that it was as if my heart leaped out towards him and I held his hand tightly.

'Oh, I know,' I agreed quickly. 'It's just . . . .'

I hesitated and when I glanced at him I saw that he was looking at me with a strangely speculative look. I was so anxious that I might be attaching too much importance to his attempted embrace, so infatuated was I by him, that I decided that I must be more sophisticated although I felt rather nervous. My feelings for him were almost entirely romantic and the physical side of the relationship as yet meant no more to me than holding hands and kissing. It seemed, however, that he intended to make no more advances at the moment and I was both disappointed and relieved. It was as though he had withdrawn from me and I remember that I made great efforts on the walk to the bus stop.

I suppose I should have seen the danger signals. It was a little while now since we'd been to the theatre or to a dance or to his favourite French restaurant for dinner. Rarely did he borrow his father's car. Now we walked about, stopping at coffee bars or going to the cinema and, although I had assumed that it was because we were beginning to relax and become a serious couple, I realise now that the truth of it was that Geoffrey knew that he no longer needed to make any great efforts for me. Even now I am not certain whether Ursula's arrival was the turning point or whether he was already tiring of me but I can recall the tiny expert slights and calculated actions he used to detach himself from me. Even then I was too dense to see it and he was obliged to deal the final death blow with a certain amount of brutality.

He did it at a farewell party in the restaurant. I cannot remember now who was leaving but the staff had been invited and there had been the usual collection and a present had been bought. The speeches were over and we were making the most of the free wine when Geoffrey manoeuvred me into a quiet corner. He looked rather flushed and his eyes scanned the crowd even whilst he talked to me.

'Have you guessed that I have something very important to say to you?' he asked, and for one wild glorious moment I thought he was going to propose to me.

I stared at him and he smiled a little, his eyes bright.

'I've been thinking,' he said deliberately. 'Can you guess what I've been thinking?' I shook my head dumbly, hope in my heart. 'I think that we've been seeing too much of each other.'

'Too much . . .?' I could barely understand him. '*Too* much?'

He smiled then, as if at some private satisfaction, and nodded. 'We're getting too serious, I'm sure you'll agree. After all, we're both very young. Much too young to be tying ourselves down. It would be better if we had more freedom.'

'To do what?' I asked, distressed. 'I don't need more freedom. I only want to be with you.'

He laughed a little. 'How sweet you are. But I do, you see. I think it's always best to be honest in these cases, don't you? The truth is, there's another girl I'm interested in and I want the chance to get to know her.'

I was quite silent with shock. Once again he glanced quickly across the restaurant and, following his look, I saw Ursula watching us. I guessed then – and my humiliation was complete. Pride, which had been absent for so long in my relationship with him, miraculously came to my rescue and, as the laughter and chatter ebbed and flowed around me, I was determined that I should not break down. He was watching me closely now and I was able to meet his eyes although I was afraid to risk my voice. I swallowed several times.

'If that's how you feel . . .'

He bent near to catch the words, hearing the tremor which

I could not conceal. 'I'm afraid it is.' He did not look afraid or even regretful. He looked triumphant.

I shrugged. Misery was welling up inside me and I feared it might surge out through my eyes and mouth in tears and sobs. It was Vanessa who came to my rescue.

'Thank God that's over!' She came drifting up to us, holding a glass and looking as beautiful as ever. 'Don't look so dismal, darling. It's not *that* bad. Let's disappear, shall we? Come and have some coffee at Mario's.'

Geoffrey slipped past her and disappeared into the crowd. She raised her eyebrows at me.

'Did I break something up?'

I shook my head and then nodded. I felt my lips tremble and she took my arm and steered me out through the door and into the body of the store.

'Come on,' she said. 'Fetch your coat. Let's get out of here.'

I was too miserable to protest and presently we were in Mario's coffee bar with an espresso before us. It took Vanessa no time at all to worm it all out of me and her reaction was probably the best tonic I could have had at that moment.

'But he's such a boring little man, darling,' she said, lighting a cigarette and looking amazed that I should be the least bit concerned by his defection. 'I never could understand your passion for him. Completely second rate.'

My lips shook a little and I lifted my cup so as to disguise this. She surveyed me thoughtfully through wreaths of smoke and I knew that I should have defended Geoffrey. I felt disloyal and then, remembering what he had done to me, I became confused and even more miserable. Vanessa shook open her cigarette packet and offered me one. I shook my head and she gestured impatiently.

'For goodness' sake! Have one and cheer up. Tell you what. Why don't we go and see a flick? You don't want to sit and mope. Or perhaps we'll try that new disco . . . Hang on. I'm going to make a few telephone calls . . . .'

So it began. I remember how indignant the Carols and Lorraine were at my apparent defection. They were not pleased that I had gone off with 'the enemy' without so much as a word and I was obliged to sacrifice my pride to our friendship and tell them the whole story. They were so shocked by Geoffrey's behaviour that they forgave me instantly and I was immediately surrounded by their sympathy and support. Lorraine declared that she would never speak to him again and forbade Mrs Cotton to be anything but icily polite. Mrs Cotton, like a good many others, had guessed how it would end but there was one positive outcome. The sight of Geoffrey; lingering on the stairs, hurrying past the cosmetic counter, tarrying outside the restaurant, made me long for the moment when I could avoid this daily humiliation and move up to the fifth floor.

6

The fact that Elizabeth Ferrars and I hit it off surprisingly well together is at the root of my guilt. Had I been more mature, less impressionable, that final terrible scene need never have been enacted. She was cautious to begin with, of course. She knew of my relationship with David Eastwell and was prepared to be wary of me. I, however, was so glad to be away from the gossiping tongues and sympathetic glances of the ground floor staff – not to mention the spectacle of Geoff's pursuit of Ursula – that I was determined to give of my best. I had to start all over again. Working in the china and glass department was nothing like haberdashery. We had very few customers and nearly all the items we sold were sent down to the packing department either to be collected or delivered. Our customers demanded a certain amount of knowledge and often wished to wade through the catalogues which we kept in the department. I recognised certain names; Wedgwood, Royal Doulton, Waterford. Now I had to learn to recognise designs and patterns. The department also sold lampshades and wall lights and tea trolleys.

I was assigned the small desk next to the large glass-fronted erection behind which Elizabeth Ferrars spent most of her working hours; Sancho Panza to her Boanerges. I dusted the glass shelves and the china and glass, mugged up on the designs and looked forward to Mr Dickson's visits. Mr Dickson was the window dresser assigned to the fifth floor who, accompanied by an acne-ridden youth of some sixteen summers, would appear at regular intervals to collect items for his displays in the 'dining rooms' or 'bedrooms' or 'sitting rooms' either in the window display or elsewhere in the furniture departments. He had to sign a little book to show which things he had taken; two Doulton figurines, 'Diana' and 'Autumn Breezes', one set of Waterford Crystal wine goblets, an onyx table lamp with a green silk shade – and so on. Off they would go, the two of them, clutching these items or pushing them on one of the expensive trolleys.

'Do be careful!' Elizabeth Ferrars would cry as she watched them bumping the tiny wheels over the ridged entrance to the lift, china clinking against glass, the table lamp wobbling precariously.

Her tone suggested, quite accurately, that she resented anything being taken from the department. So did I – but for quite different reasons. Should a customer wish to see an item which was out on display I was the one sent off to find it; toiling up and down the stairs – staff were not allowed to use the lifts lest we contaminate a customer – or round the endless acres of carpeted floor until I found the little figurine stuck on a dressing table in the beds department. I would seize it and go hurrying back – 'Try to be quicker next time, Marchant, nearly lost that customer. People get tired of waiting, you mustn't dawdle!' – warding off Mr Burrage, an ancient salesman, who, with his weak eyesight, often mistook me for a shoplifter. Elizabeth Ferrars would be entertaining the customer; catalogues all over the glass counter; stock taken down to illustrate a point. Afterwards I would be the one to put them all away.

Elizabeth Ferrars. I can still picture her quite clearly. I thought her old – well, certainly middle-aged – but she was probably no more than thirty-eight. She was very fastidious. Her shirts – plain and simple – were always immaculate: her skirts – practical – were well-pressed: her shoes – sensible – were highly polished. She wore the minimum of make-up – enough powder so as not to shine and a hint of pale lipstick – and her short dark hair was always in place. It was impossible to imagine her as passionate, wild, frantic – or, at least, it was in the beginning.

She had a light, slightly sarcastic manner to me, rather like a schoolmistress with a pupil, and her habit of addressing me by my surname underlined that impression. When she saw that I was disposed to be friendly she thawed slightly and began to teach me the stock. It was evident that she loved the pieces which she held with a kind of tenderness, showing me the difference in shape and design. Even now – often to my hostess's consternation – I find that I am turning over a plate to see the maker's name and am delighted if I have guessed correctly. I run my fingers over my wineglass and try to hazard if it is a piece of Webb Corbett or Edinburgh crystal. She taught me a great deal.

I was too absorbed, to begin with, to be aware of the atmosphere about me. That she was unpopular, I already knew. As to why, I accepted the reasons which Lorraine had already explained to me. She was standoffish and stuck up and she had been given the department over the head of Brenda Grice.

Brenda Grice. I can picture her, too. Fat, fair and forty and with a bubbly charm that disguised the thinness of her lips and the calculating coldness of the pale blue eyes. This, of course, is with hindsight. At the time I was flattered by her friendliness. As far as I could see she was employed mainly in soft furnishings with Mr Fullivant but she helped out with anyone who was short-staffed; strutting between the departments on high-heeled shoes, her ample bottom encased in short skirts chosen to display plump calves in shiny stockings. She was very popular with the men. I had seen her in the canteen but, although she waved encouragingly from soft furnishings, she didn't approach me. I waved back, one eye on Elizabeth Ferrars' bent head.

'I don't want you gossiping with other members of staff,' she had told me almost at once. 'We're rather isolated up here and silly feuding goes on. Whose figures are the highest and so on. What happens in this department is absolutely confidential. Please understand that. Also Mrs Grice and Mr Griffiths waste a great deal of time gossiping. Please don't encourage them.'

I understood why people disliked her. She made the mistake of letting them see that she thought herself superior to them. Well, she was. She went out to coffee or lunch without looking to right or left, walking briskly, head held high. As soon as she had disappeared down the stairs the whispering would begin. In those early days I was left well alone; perhaps no one knew whose side I was on or perhaps they feared what I might say to a higher authority. Nevertheless, I watched them gather on the edge of their departments, saw their glances at me. There was Mr Griffiths from the bedding department which lay beyond the high wall of our display shelves, Mrs Grice, of course, with Mr Fullivant, and one of the furniture salesman, Mr Baxter. I longed to join them.

Mr Griffiths was one of the funniest men I had ever met. He and Mr Baxter were old friends, both Londoners, and their humour was irresistible. It was lonely and quiet on the fifth floor and the sound of Griff and Bax joshing always drew me to the entrance way – if Elizabeth Ferrars happened to be out. It was only later that I realised that there was a cruelty to Griff's humour. He could smell out the people who came in to avoid the rain or to waste time and he was quite brutal to them. I can see him now, advancing on just such a woman who had already been round china and glass and now moved into soft furnishings. He watched her, rubbing his hands together over and over as if he were anticipating a treat. Presently he approached her.

'May I help you, Madam?' he asked.

He had a peculiarly menacing smile, I remember. He never opened his lips and it did not touch his eyes. His thin silvery hair was always plastered to his scalp and he wore a grey pinstripe suit. The woman was riffling half-heartedly through a pile of quilts and she straightened up.

'No, no thank you,' she said, a little nervously. 'I'm looking for a friend, actually.'

'Well, you won't find her in there, Madam,' said Griff, still smiling.

I remember hiding behind a display cabinet as I stifled my laugher. We had lots of laughs together when Elizabeth Ferrars was out. Nevertheless, I missed my friends from the ground floor. I still saw them occasionally in the canteen but it wasn't quite the same. I hardly ever saw Little Carol or Lorraine any more. For some reason, Elizabeth Ferras liked to take early coffee and lunch breaks and I found myself promoted to much more civilised times. Sadly these did not coincide with those of my friends and gradually we began to drift apart. When we did manage to get together the old magic was missing. Perhaps I didn't make quite as much effort as I might have done because, at this time, my friendship with Vanessa was ripening.

True to her word, she had introduced me to some of her gang. Like her they were easy-going, fun-loving and very well-heeled. They took me in with casual friendliness and I discovered that it was fun to be part of a group. I was still suffering from Geoff's defection and deliberately avoided the ground floor so as not to have to see Ursula. Then, to my distress, she decided that her affection for Geoff was greater than her desire to eat in the restaurant and she took to coming into the canteen. The sight of them sitting together, and his sly glances at me, was too much for my hard-won composure. I dropped in to see Vanessa in the boutique and grizzled about it as I worked my way along the rails.

'Oh, honestly, darling!' She looked despairingly at me. 'You're not *still* pining over that drip! I thought you were doing rather well the other night with Henry.'

'It was fun,' I admitted. 'He's nice. But that doesn't mean that I want to see Geoff all over that cow from cosmetics.'

Vanessa chuckled and then shrugged. 'I keep telling you,' she said. 'You should go out. Pop over to Mario's. No one would notice and who cares if they do? You can say you had a dental appointment.'

'In a coffee bar?'

'It was such a grim experience that you needed a restorative drink,' improvised Vanessa. 'You'll think of something. Anyway, no one will see you. Bet you! Come out with me at lunchtime, why don't you? We go at the same time now, don't we? Go on! Be a devil!'

I can't remember what made me take up her challenge. Perhaps it was the long dull hours, unpunctuated by gossips with the Carols or seeing the others in the canteen, that made me feel restless enough to take the risk. Perhaps I was still so miserable about Geoff that I didn't much care if I got into trouble. I only remember that I went.

My preoccupation with the past delays me and I have only just finished washing up my breakfast things when a friend drops by for a discussion about a charity bazaar. I have completely forgotten that I invited her but I manage to cover my confusion and we drink many cups of coffee whilst we thrash out the details. It is as she is leaving that we see the morning's post lying on the hall floor and she bends to pick up the envelopes.

'Oh, how nice. A letter from abroad.' She hands me the blue envelope. 'Why does an airmail letter seem much more exciting than an ordinary one?'

I am too busy examining the writing to hazard an answer to her question. The letter comes from Vanessa's region in France but it is not her writing on the envelope. I turn it to look at the sender's name and see that it is from Alex. I hurry my friend out of the door and down the path, waving enthusiastically as she climbs into her car and drives away. I shut the front door and tear open the envelope, already reading his letter as I make my way back to the kitchen. Alex is not a good correspondent – although we always have exchanged birthday and Christmas cards – and it is odd to have this communication from a boy of twenty-two or three, writing to me as though we are old friends.

'Dear Fiona and James' he writes – there was never any nonsense about calling us 'aunt' or 'uncle' or even 'godfather' – and the tone of the letter reminds me of Vanessa,

'I can't wait to see you next week. Maman says that she's sure you'll be quite happy to put me up and I'm longing to come. It seems years and years since we met – well, it is, of course! Maman's been telling me all about when you were all young and she's getting quite sentimental and maudlin about it. I tell her that she should come with me but she says that both of us would be too much of a shock!! I must say that it sounds a lot of fun that you had in the good old sixties. I feel quite envious! She sends her love to you both . . . .'

I pause, surprised that Vanessa should be capable of sentimentality. She is such a person for living in the present. However, the older we get the more prone we are to look back at the past which, for some, seems bathed in an eternal glow of sunshine. They *were* magic days; slipping out for those lunchtime picnics, driving to the coast on Sundays, dancing until early morning . . . What a shock it was when Vanessa and Tony decided to split up. James was reluctant to discuss it and went down to the farm when Vanessa and Alex came to stay for a few days. I think that James felt that his loyalty was to Tony and that it would have been difficult for him to cope with the situation without hurting her. I know that he always believed that Vanessa trapped Tony into marriage by getting pregnant. Vanessa was evasive about the reasons for the divorce. During her stay she was her usual casual self, seeming almost indifferent to her situation, yet I sensed that there was something she wanted to tell me. I was very sad. Vanessa and Tony were part of *us* and the small Alex was enchanting. Blond and blue-eyed like Tony, he also displayed some of his mother's easy charm and friendliness. I adored him.

I remember that, when we weren't discussing the divorce, I told her about my problems; that I was unable to conceive. She sat on my sofa her long thin, elegant legs stuck out before her, her eyes on Alex, playing on the rug.

'If it comes to the worst, darling,' she said with her old insouciance, 'we'll have to share Alex.'

I laughed – I didn't truly believe that I would never have a child or, that having her, would lose her so tragically – and bent to pull Alex on to my lap.

'When you get tired of him,' I said, kissing his rosy cheek, 'send him along.'

Now, twenty years later, she is doing just that. Holding his letter I try, yet again, to understand why we all drifted apart. We could have visited Vanessa in France; we could have spent weekends with Tony. With broken marriages come divided loyalties. It is hard to remain friends with both sides and James and I were already on different sides. Tony married again quite quickly and is the father of a large family.

Vanessa has had several lovers and has recently married a Frenchman. Perhaps a twenty-two-year-old boy is rather a handicap to a new marriage and Vanessa is relieved to send Alex back to England, knowing we will keep an eye on him. If only James were not so sensitive . . . .

I reject the idea of keeping Alex's visit a secret. We must all face up to new beginnings. I realise that I am longing to see him and that he must be assured of a warm welcome and, going to my bureau, I prepare to write to him hoping that my letter will arrive before he sets out.

The letter written it is only right that James should now be told. It is Friday and this evening we are going to dinner with friends. Deviously I decide that whilst we are getting ready will be a good moment to broach the subject. There will hardly be time for an argument and James is far too good-mannered to vent his spleen on his hosts. I wonder if this might be the moment to talk more openly about Sarah. The familiar pain thrills through me. She would be eighteen now; a pretty, bright, happy girl, bringing home boyfriends, going to parties. Perhaps she and Alex . . . I pull myself together. I have trained myself to avoid such thoughts. As I potter about, brushing James's dark suit, pressing my long skirt, I remember the tremendous joy with which he greeted the long awaited news. Had he longed for a child so much? Or did he feel guilty lest I should never conceive? But, after all, it might have been just as much my fault as his. Oh, he was so proud, so tender, so caring! It was just as well that he was obliged to be at the office all day or I should have never been allowed to move for the whole nine months.

'. . . *delighted to hear that you are in pig, at last*!' Vanessa wrote in reply to my ecstatic letter. '*Give James my congratulations. He certainly took his time! Tell him that I expect him to be quicker off the mark next time . . . .*'

Foolishly I let him see her letter, too happy to take her

remarks seriously. I had made no allowances for James's sensitivities, however, and I saw his face flush and his brows draw together. It was another black mark against her and I regretted my tactlessness. Anyway, there was no next time. Somehow it seemed unimportant that no more children followed Sarah. She was all that we had longed for and much, much more . . . In my head I hear the screech of brakes, the crash of tangling metal, the screams of the trapped children, and I hurry to switch on the radio, tearing my mind away from the agony. No. I shall not be able to talk with James about her death. How could either of us bear it?

I think instead of Elizabeth Ferrars. Were there any signposts that I missed? Any indications which I ignored? Quite suddenly I am reminded of the almost uncontrollable anger with which she confronted me when I returned from one of those delicious picnics. I sit down on the end of the bed, smoothing the velvet of my long evening skirt and trying to recall which picnic it was. Was it the first? I think it was just the three of us; Vanessa, Tony and me. It had been arranged on the spur of the moment . . . Yes, it is coming back to me now. . . .

Things were improving in the china and glass department. I think that Elizabeth Ferrars was beginning to trust me, even to like me a little. She saw that I made no attempt to fraternise with the others and she began to be more friendly. Imperceptibly we began to work as a team and, occasionally, she asked me questions about myself, my education, my home life. My answers must have chimed with the opinions she had already formed and, as the weeks passed, she began to relax, teasing me, joking a little with me.

'Come on, Marchant,' she'd say. 'Get the duster out,' and she'd pull my leg about my being a member of the privileged classes.

'I thought that I might die laughing,' she told me, 'the first time I saw you attempting to put a lamp shade into a paper bag. Have you *ever* been asked to do anything useful?'

I laughed with her and told her Little Carol's version of my debacle with the customer and her 'two fingers.'

'Honestly,' she shook her head, chuckling. 'You shouldn't be let out without a keeper.'

Now that the pain was wearing off I even told her about Geoff. She frowned, her eyes thoughtful.

'Good-looking young man? Dark and thin? Yes, I've seen him about. Rather *pleased* with himself, wouldn't you say? Has a smug look about him.'

She sounded like Vanessa and I felt rather disconsolate. 'I suppose so,' I admitted grudgingly, feeling that I had been a fool to be taken in by him. She touched me lightly on the shoulder. 'You can do better than Geoff from travel goods,' she said gently and I felt a rush of affection for her. I smiled at her gratefully but she turned away immediately, drawing my attention to some neglected piece of work, and the moment passed. There were enough such moments to give me the courage to defend her when her detractors criticised her to me but, even then, I found her attitude of 'them and us' faintly irksome. I was young enough to be attracted by the gossip and jokes of Brenda Grice and Griff and Bax. Elizabeth Ferrars gave the impression that the department was in some way sacred; the last stronghold of Christianity, besieged constantly by the infidel beyond its walls and I found it faintly ridiculous. Oddly, though, I found myself wanting to please her, even to protect her from the watchful eyes outside. There was something about her; a kind of desperate courage, a quality of character that contemptuously rejected the *double entendres* of Griff and Bax and the smutty asides of Brenda Grice. Most of these, I must admit, simply went over my head. I think it was not unusual, even then, for a young girl to be naive and they seemed to have such fun, the three of them.

Brenda Grice had a boyfriend. It was Griff who told me and it came as the most dreadful shock. It had not occurred to me that married women *could* have boyfriends and I was confused, even anxious. He enjoyed telling me: his eyes fixed slyly on my face, as if they would extract every nuance of my reaction, his hands rubbing and rubbing away. I know now that he was the sort of person who delights in shattering youth's illusions, discrediting his friends, revelling in a lowering of moral standards and, all the while, making it sound tremendous fun and perfectly reasonable. How insidic us and dangerous such people are! I instinctively knew that my innocent disapproval would be gently derided, censure would be affectionately mocked, and, anyway, I imagined that he was treating me as one of the lads and I felt grown-up and important. I am quite certain that the devil is of the Griff variety; not at all a frightening person but an intimate voice at one's ear making one laugh, albeit guiltily, and smoothing one's weaknesses and vanities into acceptable virtues. I think one of his most tempting encouragements to self-indulgence would be the phrase, 'after all, you're only human . . . .'

It was quite amazing how quickly I moved from shock, at Griff's disclosures, to acceptance, even to a certain amount of admiration at Brenda Grice's worldly sophistication. I have to admit to a private derision at the use of the word 'boyfriend'. After all, Brenda Grice was forty if she was a day! When this 'boyfriend' appeared in the store shortly afterwards I was dumbfounded. He was at least fifty-five and grey into the bargain! Nevertheless it was all great fun, jolly jokes and so on, and I was introduced. Needless to say, Elizabeth Ferrars was at lunch. He looked me over with prominent, assessing eyes and I felt a slight inward shuddering, as though a snail had crawled across me leaving a trail of sticky slime. I glanced at Brenda Grice, who was watching me consideringly, and she laughed.

'Poor child,' she said to – his name escapes me. 'Much too pretty to be cooped up in here, isn't she?'

He continued to appraise me whilst Griff stood off, smiling, always smiling, whilst his hands rubbed softly together, turning and twisting in anticipation.

'Where's the Gorgon?' the boyfriend asked easily. 'Gone to Mass, has she? Nipped out for a lunchtime quickie with the priest?'

It was the first intimation I'd had that Elizabeth Ferrars was a Roman Catholic. I laughed with Brenda Grice and Griff, too afraid of appearing stuck-up or naive not to, but all at once I felt another sense of revulsion at the almost indecent sensualism that emanated from Brenda and her boyfriend. It was as though they had a secret which they were prepared to share with me – on their terms. Part of the price was a betrayal of Elizabeth Ferrars and her standards but I was already ashamed at my disloyalty and of the weakness which encouraged me to seek their acceptance and approval at her expense. To my relief, a customer came into the department and I was obliged to turn away.

Afterwards I considered the idea of Elizabeth Ferrars being a Roman Catholic. I recalled a conversation we'd had regarding abortion and how unusually heated she'd become, saying that it was a crime; murder even. I was too ignorant and untaught to be able to maintain an intelligent discussion on the subject but it was quite clear that she felt very strongly about it and I was disturbed to see the usually cool contained woman speaking with such vehemence. If she were indeed a Roman Catholic it would explain her passionately held views.

It was at about this time that I met Tony. I had become quite hardened by now to slipping out at lunchtime with Vanessa. Her casual confidence infected me and, in her company, I was able to be more daring. She swept me along with her, keeping an eye on me – as far as her natural indolence would allow. On this particular day, with Elizabeth Ferrars back at her desk, I hurried down the stairs and into the boutique.

'Oh, hell!' She was inspecting herself in the small glass of her powder compact and she looked sideways at me guiltily.

'What's the matter? Aren't we going out today?' It never occurred to me to take the decision. It was simpler to allow her to lead and for me to follow.

She meditated, a finger against her lips, her eyes fixed unseeingly on my face. 'The thing is . . .' she paused and then seemed to make up her mind. 'Never mind. You'll just have to come along, too. Why not?'

'Come along where? What's happened?'

'I've met this rather divine man,' she said, rapidly collecting her things and sweeping me out of the boutique with a smiling nod to the girl who relieved her. 'Last night at Jimmie's. He invited me on a picnic and I thought it might be rather fun. And it's a perfect day for it!'

'But Vanessa!' I hung back, horrified. 'I can't possibly come with you. He hasn't invited *me*.' I could well imagine the disappointment of this unknown young man. 'I simply can't!'

'Absolute rubbish, darling!' She seized my arm and we clattered down the back stairs together. 'He's not at all that sort of chap!'

'What sort of chap?' I asked breathlessly.

'Oh, you know! The pouncing, heavy sort of chap. He's just the most tremendous fun. He won't mind, I promise you.'

I knew that this was another of her generous gestures. She would risk her own amusement – and that of the young man – rather than expose me to the sight of Geoff and Ursula canoodling in the canteen. She knew that I lacked the courage to go out by myself. We fled out of the staff entrance, hurrying round the nearest corner like a couple of escapees, and pulled up short. At the kerb stood a long, beautiful sports car in racing green and at the wheel, idly smoking a cigarette, lounged a long, beautiful man. He turned his head and saw us and with a gracefully controlled movement, he swung himself over the low door and came to meet us. If he were distressed at the idea of having a third on his picnic he gave no sign of it. His manners were impeccable and he seemed as idly confident and relaxed as Vanessa herself. He shook my hand warmly and moved the hamper into the boot. Giggling, Vanessa climbed in and perched on the small back seat, leaning forward to give Tony – for it was he – a quick hug.

'What fun,' she murmured, her lips to his ear. 'Got a ciggie, darling?'

I felt embarrassed that Vanessa should have taken the narrow uncomfortable seat rather than the comfortable leather covered bucket affair into which I sank but my protests were swiftly overborne. I saw that Vanessa was enjoying herself mightily, earning the whistles and attention of the young males at traffic lights and zebra crossings, as she displayed her legs in their sheer tights – a new innovation to compliment the daring miniskirt – and squeaking with pleasure as the car roared away, flinging her backwards as she waved saucily to her admirers.

Tony seemed to be enjoying it just as much as she was. Covertly I studied him. He was tall; his legs in immaculate flannels seemed to go on forever – just like the bonnet of his car – and his hands, negligently disposed on the steering wheel, had thin long fingers. His face was bony, his nose beaky, and his good-humoured blue eyes gazed out placidly at the world. His fair hair was sleek and well-cut; his flannel shirt sported a silk scarf at the throat. I knew at once that I was in the presence of the genuine article and, consequentially, felt rather shy of him but there was no need. He behaved as though my presence was a bonus to the party and soon I began to relax. He drove us to one of the city's green parks and soon the thick soft wool rug was spread and the picnic unpacked. To me it was the ultimate in style; cold roast chicken, hot rolls wrapped in napkins, strawberries and cream . . . and wine: chilled white wine poured into long crystal glasses. How could I have resisted? Afterwards there was strong delicious black coffee from a thermos and, after that, Tony insisted that we had a nip of brandy poured into the silver top of his hip flask. Giggling and choking we complied before we were swept back, singing and laughing, to Winslow's. Vanessa was much more used to this sort of thing than I and I made my entrance into the department more ebulliently than was wise. Elizabeth Ferrars watched me gain my desk and stood up, staring down at me, frowning.

'You've been drinking, Marchant!' Her tone was clipped, her expression disgusted.

I began to giggle, thought the better of it and hiccupped. 'Sorry,' I said blithely.

'Brandy. I can smell it on your breath.' Her face contracted with distaste. 'Where did you get it?'

Common sense made a belated entry 'It . . . it was someone's birthday,' I lied. Naturally she assumed that I had been in the canteen.

'Oh, really!' She seemed overcome. 'To give brandy to a girl of your age . . .' She seemed almost as moved as she had been by the abortion question. 'Go down to the canteen and get yourself some coffee. Go on. Be quick!'

I hurried out of the department, away from her disapproval – and from something else. Griff was standing just outside the entrance, close up to the dividing wall, eavesdropping. I caught his expression; the long, thin lips stretched in the usual smile; his eyes avid, puzzled. I smiled foolishly as I dashed past him, feeling ashamed and resentful all at the same time. After all, it was hardly a crime to have a tiny sip of brandy after lunch . . . Yes, the signs were there but I had neither the wit nor the experience to read them.

The sound of James's voice calling in the hall makes me jump and I glance at my watch in horror. He is home early. I throw my skirt on to the bed and hurry down to him. Now is the time for talk, to show him Alex's letter, to reconcile him to the idea of his godson's imminent arrival. We may not be able to show our own wounds to each other but we must no longer treat Alex – or Vanessa for that matter – as a scapegoat for our grief. As I run down the stairs I am aware of a great relief that he is early. There will be time for a glass of whisky, maybe two, before I broach the subject; something to edge him into a receptive mood; to soften the news and make it acceptable to him.

8

He sits with his head resting against the wing of the chair; legs stretched out to the fire; tilting the whisky gently in its glass. His horn-rimmed spectacles have always lent him an academic air and, indeed, in his family he is always referred to as the 'clever' one. His love for reading, his ability to pass exams and win scholarships, a more serious approach to life, set him slightly apart. It was the same within our little group. It was always James who restrained us, cautioned us from being too noisy, too risky, too excessive. It was clear that Tony was very fond of him and took this in good part. Vanessa chose to tease him; she called him 'Nanny'.

It was quite early on when I began to recognise signs of approaching danger. When he is anxious James had – still has – the habit of almost snatching his spectacles from his face, seizing the frame between finger and thumb and holding them at arm's length, elbow resting on knee or on the arm of a chair. With his free hand he would rub his eyes and massage the bridge of his nose. I cannot remember when I first noticed this habit of his but I began to watch for it, ready to distract him. He does it still, often when he is thinking about Sarah, when he is overcome by frustration, distress, anger. I am watching for it this evening.

'I've had a letter from Alex,' I remark when James is into his second drink. I have decided to leave Vanessa out of it. 'He's got an interview at the university here. They've offered him a place on a post-graduate course and he's very excited about it.'

James sits quite still, his eyes fixed on the flames. He remains silent and I prattle on.

'He can't wait to get back to England and I must say I'm looking forward to seeing him.'

James looks at me. 'Seeing him?'

'Why yes,' I reply casually. 'I've offered to put him up. Naturally.'

Off comes the spectacles! 'Naturally?' He sets his glass on the table beside his chair.

'Oh, come on James!' I allow a hint of impatience to creep into my voice. 'He's your godson. Vanessa is one of our oldest friends. The university is barely twenty minutes away. Of course we must invite him to stay. He's longing to meet you again.'

I know this flattery will have little or no effect but throw it in for good measure. James's eyes are closed and he massages the bridge of his nose almost desperately. I ache with pity for him, knowing how he has allowed Alex to become the scapegoat of his grief for Sarah, knowing his thoughts. *Why should this child live whilst mine dies? Why should Vanessa go free while I suffer?* Thus has his pain and frustration been disseminated. I hear the music of the dance, the warning – if muffled – drumbeat, and fear lest we should be swept apart.

'Darling.' I kneel beside his chair and take his hand tightly in mine. 'Don't you think it's time we tried to talk? *Really* talk.' I feel his hand move convulsively in my grasp. 'I hate this feeling of distance between us. I know why you avoid the subject. Of course I do. I'm not an idiot.'

James stiffens, staring at me. There is a wary, puzzled look in his eyes and I know that he is surprised that I have brought it into the open at last. I dare to go a little further.

'It's so easy to feel resentful,' I say carefully, 'but isn't it time to let it all go now? Resenting Alex won't bring Sarah back. After all it's not *his* fault.'

After a long, very long, moment James relaxes and gives a deep, deep sigh. I continue to clutch his hand and he returns the pressure. I hear the threatening drumbeat recede. Or perhaps it is simply the reverberation of my blood pounding in my head.

'Very well,' he says. His voice is resigned – and something else, relieved perhaps? – and he sounds very tired. 'Perhaps you're right. Let him come then.'

I sit back on my heels, surprised and gratified at such an easy victory. Was this all that has been needed to break down the barrier between us? I look at him, willing him to show that he, too, has been affected in some way. He smiles, squeezes my hand briefly and picks up his glass.

'I'd better go and change,' he says.

I get off my knees, feeling rather foolish now, and sit back in my chair as he swallows the last of his whisky and goes upstairs. Have I achieved anything? Alex will come to stay but will that reservation continue to exist between me and James? Despite his capitulation I feel that I am still being held away from him. As I rinse the glasses and climb the stairs, I am thinking of my first meeting with James.

By the time Elizabeth Ferrars' annual leave was due, she and I had evolved a very reasonable working relationship. I confined my fun with Brenda Grice and with Griff and Bax to the periods when she was out of the department and worked hard at learning my new job. The hours seemed long. Customers were few and far between, although they bought extensively when they appeared, and one could spend only limited time dusting and polishing. I sat at my small desk, studying catalogues, my ears pricked for the whispers and stifled mirth which drifted in from the other departments. My trips down to the dispatch department in the basement assumed the aura of tiny outings which relieved the boredom and I took as long as I dared preparing the appropriate dockets and bearing the precious pieces down in the goods lift.

It was on one of these 'outings' when I bumped into Geoff – almost literally. He was coming out of dispatch, chin on shoulder, talking to someone inside, whilst I rounded the corner from the lift clutching some breakable object. We collided and I shrieked with terror as the glasses – yes! I remember now that is was a consignment of Waterford Crystal on its way to be packed up – rattled madly together on their tray. Geoff reached out to steady them and one hand covered mine on the handle of the tray whilst the other silenced the tinkling, ringing crystal.

'How are you?' He made no attempt to move his hand but smiled down at me. 'I haven't seen you about. I've missed you.'

This was difficult to believe except as an audience to his new affair to which, no doubt, my presence had added a certain piquancy. I longed to tell him that I went out at lunchtimes, in long-nosed sports cars, and ate chicken and strawberries and drank wine but knew that this would be unwise. As it happened it was also unnecessary.

'I hear that you've found a rather glamorous chauffeur.'

He watched me alertly and I wondered who his informant could possibly be. Whoever it was, the news had obviously re-awakened his interest in me – or perhaps his pursuit of Ursula had reached its natural end. I managed a cool smile and raised my eyebrows but I remained silent. He frowned a little and his hand tightened on mine.

'I really meant it, you know.' His voice was lowered now, more intimate. 'I've missed you. I've been hoping to see you but you're very elusive these days.'

'It was you who wanted more freedom,' I reminded him

tartly and then regretted this unconsidered remark. Already he was smiling a little and yes, Elizabeth Ferrars was quite right, he *did* look pleased with himself. I made an attempt to extricate myself but he held on.

'I think I made a mistake,' he said. 'I *know* I did. Is there any possibility that you might forgive me, Fiona?'

Despite the intervening weeks I was not immune to his charm but I had enough sense to retain my self-respect.

'There's nothing to forgive,' I said with an insouciance which Vanessa might have envied. 'All over and done with.'

I made a more determined attempt to regain control of the tray and he looked hurt, almost sulky.

'I didn't realise you could be so hard,' he murmured and I nearly laughed aloud.

'Meet the new Fiona!' I exclaimed lightly.

'I preferred the old one better,' he said pettishly.

'I bet you did!' I muttered to myself as I swung away from him and pushed open the door to the dispatch department with my shoulder, giving him a brilliant smile as I went. I was pleased with my part in the exchange and later, when I went for my afternoon break, I was delighted to see Lorraine downing a quick cup of tea. We greeted each other enthusiastically and I felt another pang of guilt as I thought of my disloyalty. How easily I had jettisoned my old friends! Hoping in some way to make amends – and knowing that she would enjoy the gossip – I told her about my interchange with Geoff.

'Cheek!' she said indignantly. 'He's finished with her. Didn't take long, did it? She spends all day mooning about looking like a sick cow. Honestly! He ought to carry a public health warning. Don't you be taken in again, will you?'

I shook my head, touched by her caring, my guilt increasing. ''Course I won't! Listen, I'm sorry I don't see much of you anymore. It's just I don't seem to have my breaks at the same time . . . .'

She was shrugging philosophically, preparing to go. 'Can't be helped. Anyway, seems like you've got some new friends. Posh ones.' She grinned, delighted at my open-mouthed surprise. 'Mrs Cotton saw you when she was coming back from lunch. In a great big sports car, she said.'

So that explained how Geoff knew. Mrs Cotton would have probably taken great pleasure in telling him. I smiled, remembering Lorraine's romantic streak.

'Don't tell anyone,' I pleaded, praying that she would not ask me any questions.

'As if I would!' she said scornfully. 'Gotta go. See you.'

I sipped my tea thoughtfully and was not terribly surprised when Geoff put his head round the canteen door. He pretended surprise at seeing me and went to collect a cup of tea. I sat on serenely, determined not to be flustered.

'My luck's certainly in today,' he said, sliding into the seat opposite. He studied me whilst I pretended nonchalance. I wasn't *quite* so impervious to him as I would have wished. 'I really *am* sorry,' he was beginning in a low voice when the door opened to admit Ursula. Her eyes, large and brown and hurt, fixed on him at once and, as he smothered an exclamation of annoyance, I swallowed the last of my tea and slipped out. I ran up the stairs with a certain amount of elation. My self-esteem was somewhat restored and I was looking forward to the party to which Vanessa and I were going later that same evening. My high spirits lasted me through the afternoon and well into the evening. Vanessa and I changed in the changing room at the back of the boutique and went to have a bite to eat in Mario's. It was here that Tony found us, another young man in tow.

'Thought you'd be here,' he said to us, raising his hand in greeting to Mario, the Italian who owned the restaurant.

'Evening Mario. What are you girls drinking? Bottle of house red please, Mario.' He smiled down at us, relaxed, casual, charming. 'This is James Honeywell.' He drew James forward, his hand cupped under his elbow. 'And here are the two most beautiful girls in town, old boy. This is Vanessa. And this is Fiona.'

We shook hands and, as his fingers touched mine, I felt a strange explosion in my breast and my feelings for Geoffrey Hodge dwindled and faded as if they had never been . . . I remember everything about that evening. I remember the red and white checked table cloth and the wax-encrusted bottle which held the candle; the glasses filled with ruby red wine; my empty plate pushed aside and Vanessa's with half the food abandoned as usual. Tony picked at bits of it as she leaned against his shoulder, smoking a cigarette, her eyes sleepy, half closed, cat-like. Her small face was so perfect. The big dreamy grey-green eyes, the wide well-defined mouth, the short nose. Her heavy chestnut hair was piled elegantly on top of her head and Tony, preferring it down and loose, pulled idly at the pins. She laughed at him, lazily shaking her head so that the great weight of hair fell down over her shoulders and he ran his long thin fingers through it and buried his face in it. She smiled, never embarrassed by such displays as I should have been, and I glanced at James to see how he was reacting. He was studying them both with a quizzical expression and, catching my look, gave me a tiny wink. For a moment it seemed as if we were two adults in the presence of children and my joy soared yet higher.

The four of us stayed together at the party but already we had paired off; Vanessa and Tony; Fiona and James. We danced and our steps fitted. I remember the rumpled brightness of his hair, the way his eyes crinkled before the smile touched his lips; the breadth of his shoulders and the length of his legs. I shivered when he touched me and longed to cling to him, to drape myself about him as Vanessa did with Tony. They hardly danced; they stood, leaning together, moving languidly, embracing as they shuffled gently, slowly, round the tiny space left for dancing. Vanessa had kicked off her shoes and, with one bare arm around Tony's neck, seemed to have fallen asleep on his shoulder. I envied her her absolute confidence and her beauty which was so absolutely right for the age.

I sighed to myself – and turned as James touched my arm.

'Dance?'

I nodded . . . and so it began.

Throughout the evening my mind flips back to the past. I watch James across the breadth of polished mahogany, his head bent courteously to his neighbour. The years have been kind to him and, as he smiles, gesticulates, looks thoughtful, I see the young James; at parties, balls, rugger matches. I remember the way we were and I know that inside this grown-up, sensible Fiona, who organises bazaars, makes jam for the sale of work and helps in the coffee bar at the hospital, is the young Fiona, carefree, optimistic, passionate. I realise too how deeply Vanessa and Tony are bound up in our past. Hardly a memory is complete without them. We shared everything, laughed at the same things, went nearly everywhere together. I think that the four of us saw ourselves enclosed in a golden bubble, which we were entitled to occupy by the grace bestowed upon us by our youth and beauty. Everything must be forgiven us; everyone must love us . . . They are not long, the days of wine and roses.

Since James has been drinking rather more heavily than usual – I can guess why, I think! – I drive us home. He comes behind me as I fiddle about in the kitchen and slips his arms about me.

'I think we should talk.' His voice is muffled with

alcohol and my hair but I turn in his arms and hold him close.

'What about?' The drums are beginning again and I swallow, my throat dry now that the moment has come.

'What we were talking about earlier. You know . . .?'

We leap violently as the telephone bell shrieks out across the quiet room. James swears under his breath and, heart thudding, I run to pick up the receiver.

'Fiona? It's Philip. Is James there? Sorry to bother you so late.'

'It's OK.' Philip, James's older brother, would never telephone at this time of night unless it were an emergency. I pass the receiver to James, whispering, 'It's Philip.'

He takes it, his face grown serious, and listens without speaking for some moments. I watch him nervously, wondering what can be amiss although I am pretty sure what has happened. His answers are short and to the point and, the conversation over, he turns to me.

'Father died earlier this evening,' he says. 'Quite suddenly but with the family around him, thank God. Philip tried to get hold of us.'

'I'm sorry.' How inadequate this phrase is. 'Oh, James . . . .'

He takes my outstretched hand but his face is abstracted. 'I'll go down first thing. Thank God it's the weekend.'

'I'll come too.' I hesitate. 'I must phone Joan and Susan. We've got a coffee morning in the church hall . . . .'

'No, no.' He shakes his head, frowning. 'No need for that. There's nothing you can do and they'll have plenty on their hands organising the funeral.'

I know that Magda, Philip's capable, no-nonsense wife, will not need my brand of comfort and their daughters will be at home no doubt. I accept James's edict willingly, even thankfully and we prepare for bed, planning for tomorrow. All thoughts of intimate conversation have been swept from his mind; he is completely sober; completely preoccupied. The moment is past.

9

With James gone I am able to give myself up wholeheartedly to the joy of preparing for Alex. A tiresome chore, no doubt, for mothers whose children come and go on a regular basis, 'using the place as a hotel', but for me it is a luxury; an oft dreamed-of delight. To make up a bed, prepare a room, cook special food, buy little treats for a returning child, oh, how I have imagined it! I hear my friends complaining about just such tedious tasks and silently, whilst nodding understandingly with a smile pinned to my lips, I envy them deeply, fiercely. Inside I weep with pain and loss.

I think of my mother and wonder how she was able to be so indifferent to me, her only child. How precious were her rare, very rare, embraces; how treasured the casual endearment or word of praise. My father, attempting to soften the hurt caused by this indifference, once told me that her work was all that she required; that it was husband and child to her and that her great talent set her apart from ordinary mortals. I remember wishing that he had married one of these more ordinary mortals so that I should know a mother's love but I knew that his pride in her was enormous and that he considered the sacrifices worthwhile. His generosity made my longings seem selfish and unworthy and I tried hard to understand the fierce creative impulse that possessed her. How ironic it is that

I, who long to be a mother, should have been denied the experience except for those few short years.

Now, however, I can sweep and polish, sort out bed linen, fill and re-fill the bookcase in the small bedroom which looks west across the garden to the low line of hills. A dozen times I try to see it all with his eyes, wandering from bed to window, from window to bookcase. Downstairs I go to the kitchen to make pies and puddings with which to fill the freezer against his arrival. In five days he will be with us. Whilst I work I allow myself to drift in and out of the past, unhampered by interruption.

Just before Elizabeth Ferrars started her holiday she became noticeably agitated. She went off to see David Eastwell and returned looking grim.

'I asked him to let me leave you in charge,' she said, 'but he won't hear of it. He says that you haven't enough experience. He's putting Mrs Grice in with you.'

I opened my mouth to say 'What fun!' and shut it again quickly. With that same grim, closed expression on her face she spent all day putting things away, locking the drawers of her desk and leaving me with endless 'do's' and 'don'ts'. Brenda Grice came into the department later in the afternoon to see if there were any instructions for her. Their mutual dislike crackled tangibly beneath an icy politeness and, just round the corner, I could see Griff, rubbing his hands together, smiling to himself. That evening Elizabeth Ferrars and I left together and, as we parted on the corner, I was seized with a sudden impulse. I hugged her, saying how much I had enjoyed working with her. She did not repulse me, although a red spot burned in either cheek, and she smiled more warmly than usual, making some jocular, teasing remark. Whenever I think of her, I am glad that I made that gesture.

The next two weeks were carnival. The whole atmosphere

of the department changed. Brenda Grice's friends dropped in and other members of staff stopped off for little chats.

'You see it doesn't *have* to be like a mausoleum,' she said to me on more than one occasion. 'You poor child! We really feel for you, you know.'

I would try to be loyal to Elizabeth Ferrars with such remarks as 'Oh, she's not so bad when you get to know her,' and 'She's OK really', but Brenda Grice wouldn't have it. With an air of sympathy she would gently remind me of a surprising number of little grievances which *I* had barely noticed at the time and which surprised me. How could she possibly know of these incidents? I had not far to look for her informant. My eyes fell on Griff who seemed, these days, to live in the department; studying the pieces, reading the price labels, poking into any drawer or cupboard which had remained unlocked. I felt uneasy. How Elizabeth Ferrars would have hated this! But what could I do? How could I defend the department in my junior position? I was relieved that she had had the foresight to hide so much away. Griff and Brenda Grice rattled the drawers of her desk whilst I watched nervously, glad that I had not been entrusted with the key. I knew that against their combined weight I should have been weak enough to give it up to them.

The boyfriend appeared regularly, the prominent eyes trailing stickily over me, whilst Bax strolled in to swell the numbers and to chat to Griff who behaved as though he now had the charge of both departments. Mr Dickson would come wandering by to collect some things for his displays and would remain to joke with Brenda Grice and to sympathise with me at my unhappy situation. Even Mr Reed turned up. Mr Reed was an alcoholic who worked in beds. It was Griff – naturally – who informed me that he was an alcoholic. One quiet afternoon whilst Elizabeth Ferrars was at tea, he had shown me Mr Reed quietly sleeping it off in one of the big wardrobes. On these occasions Bax would prudently lock the door and pocket the key, lest some customer should come upon Mr Reed unawares. I was hurrying back from dispatch, worried about leaving the department unattended, when Griff appeared out of the gloom of the great furniture-filled spaces. He said a word to Bax and summoned me to him with a jerk of the chin, beckoning me into the shadowy corner. He turned the key in the lock and gently opened the door. Alarmed, I stared down at the gently snoring figure, recumbent in the wardrobe.

'Whatever is he doing?' I whispered. 'Is he ill?'

Griff smiled, rubbing and rubbing his hands. 'He's drunk,' he said softly. His eyes slid sideways to my face. 'He's an alcoholic.'

I remember that I felt frightened. Mr Reed was such a gentle inoffensive man. He always bowed when we met, his hand straying uncertainly – even indoors – to a non-existent hat, his expression vague. It had never occurred to me that he could possibly be anything but what he seemed – a polite, quiet, middle-aged furniture salesman – and to see him, flushed and snoring in the bottom of the wardrobe was another step away from childhood into the uncertainties of an adult world. It was the same sensation I had experienced when Griff told me that Brenda Grice had a boyfriend. Something in his voice, in his cunning sideways look, gave the disclosures an almost sinister meaning.

After that, I viewed Mr Reed with different eyes, feeling shy of him, and when he appeared one afternoon, weaving his way amiably into the department, I felt a thrill of fright. He was not drunk, however, just mildly intoxicated, and I remember that he bowed to me politely and offered me a pull at his hip flask, first courteously wiping the neck of the flask with a flourish of his shabby black coat sleeve. Later Griff told me that he chewed garlic in an attempt to disguise the smell of whisky, which explained the interesting and stomach-turning odour of his breath. It was evident that he rather relished the party atmosphere in the department and turned up often with his flask. I prayed that he would not do so once the holiday was over and Elizabeth Ferrars back in possession.

Imperceptibly I began to relax; it seemed foolish not to enjoy this respite. My uncomfortable feelings of loyalty began to fade a little and I started to enjoy myself. Brenda Grice was an easy-going supervisor but a good saleswoman. Her bright cheerfulness lured many an unsuspecting customer into buying and she'd wink at me when she made a sale.

'Keeps the figures up for old Fanny Ferrars,' she'd say, 'and a nice bit of commission for you.'

This was a sore point. As a buyer Elizabeth Ferrars did not earn commission. If she sold anything whilst I was out of the department she never passed the commission on to me as Brenda Grice always did. Awkwardly I suggested that, since *she* was not a buyer, she could keep the commission for herself. She laughed and patted me on the shoulder.

'I shan't miss a few bob,' she said. 'Buy yourself a mini-skirt or something. You've got the legs for it. What d'you think?' She appealed to Griff. 'Good legs for a miniskirt, hasn't she?'

I blushed, glancing at Griff. He was smiling but his eyes were on Brenda Grice's plump calves and ample bottom and he looked at me across her unsuspecting head and there was an absolute contempt in the jerk of the head he gave. Once again I was confused. His look had been unmistakable. He despised her – yet they were friends. Struggling with this new idea I tried to concentrate on Brenda Grice.

'. . . always had good legs,' she was saying, patting complacently at her blonde – her very blonde! – hair. 'Billy, that's my husband, says I could wear a miniskirt,' and, to my horror and to Griff's delight, she raised her straight knee-length skirt and displayed her thighs, bulging over stocking-tops. By the time she glanced at him his expression, compounded of disgust at the unpretty sight and pleasure that she had so degraded herself, was wiped clean from his face and he was smiling as usual, his hands rubbing and rubbing.

'Not bad for an old 'un,' he said, his eyes gleaming and she nudged him good-humouredly.

'Not so much of the "old",' she said. 'Not too old to enjoy myself!'

He nodded several times. 'You should ask Fiona to one of your parties,' he suggested with a sly wink at me.

She looked at him quickly, her face so changed and watchful that I felt embarrassed. Who was Griff to invite me to somebody else's party? I pretended to glance at my watch, muttered something about 'getting a move on' and hurried away to coffee.

Geoff was in the canteen and indicated that I should sit with him. A quick check showed that none of the old gang was present and so I collected a cup of coffee and slid into the seat opposite. Since meeting James I was utterly immune to Geoff. Is there anything deader than dead love? Not, my new wisdom told me, that I had ever loved Geoff. It had been a kind of desperate infatuation; an experiment in the ways of love perhaps, whilst I was waiting for the real thing to come along. Now that it had, Geoff was unable to move me with his renewed interest and hints at revived love. I simply did not care.

My indifference spurred him on. As had always been the case with Geoff, he desired what he could not have; the forbidden fruit would always be the sweetest. I have to say that I was not particularly kind. The brutal way he had finished our relationship made me unprepared to make any special efforts to hide my disinterest. When he saw that my reluctance was not simply an assuaging of hurt pride, he redoubled his efforts. The compliments came thick and fast and I was glad to escape from him. I dropped into the boutique on my way back to the department to find out what sort of lunchtime was planned. Vanessa had no hesitation in using the boutique's telephone for her own private use and had Megan – Winslow's telephonist – wrapped firmly round her finger.

'Picnic!' she said when she saw me. A customer, hovering at the rail, glanced inquisitively at us and Vanessa lowered her voice. 'Round the corner at five past one. Better leave separately. People are beginning to notice.'

I remembered Mrs Cotton and Lorraine and nodded. 'It's all right for you.' I told her. '*You* don't have to wear uniform. You won't be recognised so easily. Nobody in their right mind wears *this* sort of thing in the summer.'

Vanessa looked consideringly at my white shirt and black skirt. 'Grimmy, isn't it?' she agreed sympathetically. 'Can't you loosen up now you're on the fifth floor?'

'How do you mean?' I frowned at her, puzzled.

'Brenda Grice doesn't wear uniform, does she? Not as such. But *she's* not a buyer. Why don't you bend it a bit? I'm sure no one would notice. You're the only odd person out up there, aren't you, apart from Brenda?'

I could see what she was getting at and I felt tempted. 'Brenda Grice often wears grey skirts,' I said thoughtfully. 'Quite a dark grey but definitely not black . . . .'

'Well there you are then.' Vanessa sounded almost triumphant, as if she had proved a point. 'Look at this.'

'This' was a short-sleeved shift dress in grey linen. It was perfectly cut, simple and quite lovely. Vanessa swung it off the rail and held it up against herself so that I could see it. My expression obviously spoke volumes.

'So there you are.' She considered the matter settled. 'Come down a few minutes early. Brenda Grice goes after you get back, doesn't she? Well then. Come down and change into it before we go out and then keep it on for the afternoon and see how it goes. Brenda won't fuss, I promise you.'

'How do you know?' I was looking longingly at the dress but I caught the edge of her knowing grin.

'She wants you on her side,' she said cynically.

There was no time to pursue this and, anyway, I had just caught sight of the price tag.

'Gosh!' I exclaimed in dismay – but Vanessa had whisked the dress away and was hanging it inside the changing room.

'Usual terms,' she said airily. 'Credit extended indefinitely. We only live once. When you're old and fat like Brenda you'll be glad to remember that you were young and pretty and had a dress like this.'

Her words are still echoing in my head as I prepare my solitary supper. The evenings are drawing out but it is cold and I decide to eat by the fire with a tray. It is odd to be alone. James and I rarely spend any length of time apart – except for the usual working hours and those evenings when he has to work late – and there is something vaguely decadent about casually making a sandwich, collecting a piece of cheese and an apple, and carrying it into the sitting room. I pour myself a glass of wine and begin to enjoy myself. After a moment I decide to put a cassette in the machine and have some music whilst I eat. I get up and potter along looking at the row of cassettes on the shelf beside the radio. James, being several years older than the three of us, had a rather more mature taste in music. Whilst we tuned into the local pirate stations on the car radio and listened to the Top Twenty on Sunday afternoons if we could, James preferred to play his Thelonius Monk or Dave Brubeck records and he loved the old-fashioned crooners. He had Frank Sinatra's 'Songs for Swingin' Lovers' Album and he adored Peggy Lee and Ella

Fitzgerald. When we went to balls or dances, he would sing the words in my ear as we quickstepped or foxtrotted across the floor.

As I return to my chair by the fire the familiar melody catches at my heart; nothing so evocative, nothing so capable of transporting one back in time. As I eat my supper I can feel James's arms about me, his voice – half whispering, half singing – in my ear . . .

'*There may be trouble ahead but while there's moonlight and music and love and romance, let's face the music and dance . . . .*'

10

On Sunday morning James rings early. I am still fast asleep and the shrilling of the telephone bell wakes me unceremoniously from my dreams. I manage to seize the receiver, dragging my dressing gown around me, just before James hangs up. He sounds concerned and I assure him that I have just slept late – for me – and that I am perfectly fine. He talks and I listen.

Presently, having sent my love to everyone, I go to make myself coffee. Whilst yawning over the kettle I am jerked suddenly awake as James's words sink into my fuddled brain. 'The funeral will be on Friday.' And Alex is due on Wednesday evening! How dreary it will be for him to be coming into a household of mourning. How much more difficult, now, to ease James into a cheerful, welcoming frame of mind. Impatient with the complexities of life, I carry my coffee upstairs and climb back into bed. James's father is – was – a fair-minded, strict, conscientious man. Sterling qualities, these, but not qualities that readily engender love. His wife kept his stern clay soft and malleable with her gentle sweetness and ready humour but, when she died, he hardened and gradually set into a formidable figure. James and Philip have – had – a respectful affection for him but James will not miss him as he missed – still misses – his mother. I miss her, too. She answered my own aching need.

I remember the first time I met her. When James invited me down to the farm I felt that our relationship had passed into a more significant stage and, when his mother came out to greet me with a warm hug, I guessed that she, too, recognised the seriousness of the occasion. I was captivated at once by her motherliness and delighted by her readiness to accept me as one of the family. My terrors that I might not measure up to James's previous girlfriend evaporated quickly. I think that Mrs Honeywell had thought her too much of a bluestocking to feel entirely comfortable with her. I was no threat and was only too happy to potter with her in the big farmhouse kitchen, discussing recipes, or to follow her around the kitchen garden as she gathered vegetables for lunch.

In those days, James drove an old Morris Traveller. Nothing could have been further from the power and style of Tony's Triumph Roadster but I loved the Morris. I immediately felt at home in its modest interior; comfortable and relaxed as I never felt in Tony's long-nosed beast. I think that James feared that I might find his own style of living rather dull compared with Tony's charismatic progress through life. I loved to be with Tony and Vanessa, to be enjoined in their glamour and fun, but James's quieter, more homely, approach was much more appealing to me for a day-to-day existence. One cannot live continually on nectar and honeydew.

My excursions with James were the stuff of real life to me. When we went out in the Morris we talked quietly together, tentatively exchanging ideas, each slowly *learning* the other. Although he too could play the fool, he had a serious side. We went to plays and films and lent each other books. He is nearly five years older than I am and, in those days, it seemed quite a gap. He had taken a degree at university and was now studying for his chartered surveyor examinations. He told me of his love of the farm and of the country but admitted that he was glad that he had been given the opportunity to study and to widen his horizons. It seemed that, if he passed his exams, there might be an opening for him with a local firm.

My father took to him at once. James was able to hold intelligent conversations with him about finance and politics and he had a proper deference – demanded by my father, not my mother – towards my mother's work. She welcomed him absently but graciously until she discovered that he had a passion for the poetry of Gerard Manley Hopkins and then she really *saw* him. Coming upon the three of us on the terrace she would take James by the arm, smiling vaguely upon us all, and lead him away across the lawn, his bright head bent to her dark one, their voices murmuring together. My father would raise an eyebrow at me commiseratingly but I never minded. It was such heaven to be approved and acknowledged; to know that James was loved by them. Even Alma liked him. Downright praise was not just her style but her comments – 'a likely lad, that' or 'got his head screwed on' – assured me of her approval. Even the weather blessed us. The sun seemed to shine all through the summer and, looking back across the years, I see us all bathed in its beneficent glow. The summer lasted a lifetime – not just a few short weeks.

When Elizabeth Ferrars returned it was like going back to school after the holidays. I remember that my heart thumped nervously as she appeared, immaculate as ever, with no sign of a tan or other evidence of debauchery or decadent living. Brenda Grice was waiting for her and I hovered anxiously in the background as the department was, as it were, formally handed back. Perhaps I feared that my small acts of disloyalty might be reported, however innocently or unintentionally, and I heaved a private sigh of relief when Brenda Grice, with a wink at me, strutted back to soft furnishings and Mr Fullivant.

Elizabeth Ferrars gave no intimation of the former camaraderie between us and refused to talk about her holiday. She was cool and stiff and I felt oddly hurt. She set me to change the department's displays – no doubt to throw off any lingering influence left by Brenda Grice – and settled down behind her desk. As I worked, taking down dinner services and moving shelf-loads of glass, the other members of staff gave me encouraging little nods and winks. They went out of their way to pass the entrance so as to give this evidence of their solidarity and friendship and I felt as though, unintentionally, I had moved from her side to theirs.

'Shame,' whispered Brenda Grice as we passed – I on my way to the canteen, she returning from it. 'Miserable old cow! She's really taking it out on you this morning, isn't she? We had such fun, didn't we?'

'Shame,' murmured Griff when Elizabeth Ferrars had gone out to lunch, head high, looking neither to left nor right. 'Pity she didn't drown on her holiday. Brenda Grice should run your department.'

Bax, near at hand as usual, agreed with him and even Mr Reed, swaying perilously, expressed sympathy and disappointment that the halcyon days were over. After a day or two, perhaps when she realised that the department had not suffered in her absence, she unbent a little but that earlier intimacy was missing and I began to feel hard done by. Brenda Grice and Griff encouraged my feelings of dissatisfaction and, by the time the late summer sale was under way, I was seriously considering handing in my notice.

'Why should *you* be the one to go?' whispered Brenda Grice, her sharp eyes fixed on the stairs, watching for Elizabeth Ferrar's return from lunch. '*She* ought to be the one to leave, not you.'

'That's right.' Griff's eyes darted from one to the other of us, his hands rubbing and rubbing. 'I wonder you don't take it up with your friend upstairs.'

They were both looking at me now, their eyes eager, watchful.

'My friend . . .?' I stared at them stupidly. 'What friend?'

'You don't have to be coy with us.' Her tone was almost sharp but she stretched the thin lips into a smile. 'David Eastwell. Friend of yours, isn't he?'

'Oh, I see.' I laughed a little. 'He's not *my* friend. He plays golf with my father. That's how I got the job in the first place.'

'There you are then. He wouldn't want to think you were miserable, would he? Not just because of that old cow!'

I stared at them. 'But . . . but I couldn't do that, could I? It would be like . . . Well, it would be like sneaking.'

They exchanged a glance. 'It's not the same at all,' said Brenda Grice.

She sounded almost impatient but Griff continued to smile. 'The girl who was here before you, Janice Steed her name was, she left because she couldn't put up with her,' he said softly. 'It's not right. People shouldn't be allowed to be driven out of their jobs . . . .'

Elizabeth Ferrar's dark head rose in the stairwell and we fled apart. I seized my duster and plied it enthusiastically. Her voice behind me was cold.

'I've asked you not to waste time gossiping with the staff, Miss Marchant. If you haven't enough work to do please say so. I'm sure that we can remedy it.'

My cheeks burned and I could see Griff's shadow, just around the corner, where he stood listening. The day dragged by and at closing time I was glad to escape. I went down to the boutique to change. As Vanessa had foretold, Brenda Grice had made no comment about my grey linen dress apart from complimenting me on it whilst

Griff stood by, a tiny gleam of triumph in his eye. However, my nerve had failed me and, when the holiday was over, I returned to my uniform. I knew quite instinctively that Elizabeth Ferrars would not condone my grey linen dress.

Vanessa upbraided me for my feebleness of spirit but I stood firm. It was not she who had to brave the fifth floor. As I changed I bemoaned my lot and, ensconced at our usual table at Mario's, I repeated it all for the benefit of the boys. They both listened carefully but their reactions were quite different.

'I quite agree with – what d'you call 'em? – thingy and whatsit,' said Tony, lighting a cigarette. 'Go straight to the top. Get 'em to give her the push. Dreadful woman. You don't want to have to put up with that sort of thing! What d'you say, James?'

I looked at James anxiously as he turned his glass round and round, his eyes thoughtful. I hoped that his advice would be more in keeping with my own views and I was right.

'Bit drastic,' he said. 'Rushing in quite so dramatically.'

'Dear old Nanny,' murmured Vanessa. She smiled provokingly. 'Do you ever act on impulse, James?'

He coloured, not looking at her, and I felt for his knee under the table and squeezed it. He smiled at me and I felt the now familiar clutching sensation in my stomach.

'Occasionally,' he answered, still smiling at me. 'Not often. I think the real point is that Fiona isn't particularly happy at Winslow's anyway. Whoever is put in charge of the department won't matter. Am I right? Do you really feel that being a buyer for china and glass is your life's work?'

'No,' I said at once and then hesitated, hoping he wouldn't ask me what *was* my idea of my life's work. Now that I had met him I knew perfectly well but I could hardly admit it publicly.

'Then I think it would be more sensible for you to look for another job,' he said calmly. 'I'm sure your father would understand if you explain. You've given it a go.'

He found my hand and pressed it, out of sight, and my happiness seemed to well up out of my heart and threaten to choke me. Tony shrugged.

'Good idea,' he said easily, shedding his own views readily. 'Sounds much more sensible, after all. Now where can she go . . .?'

Only Vanessa took no part in these plans for my future. She continued to smile, leaning against Tony's shoulder, tilting her head to one side to blow wreaths of cigarette smoke above her head.

'And what about *my* future?' she asked plaintively at last, when my putative career had become more and more fantastic. 'What's going to happen to *me*?'

Tony put his arm around her and pulled her down to him so that her head was against his chest. He whispered in her ear and she laughed, a deep throaty laugh that somehow excited me but left me feeling naive and foolish. Why should it be that I imagined she knew so much more about life and love than I? There were times, despite her almost childish behaviour, her love of fun, that she seemed centuries older. She and Tony were so much more extravagant in their affection than were James and I, yet I believed that our love ran deeper than theirs. I looked at him and once again he sent me that tiny wink which seemed to say, 'that may *look* like the real thing but *we* know better' and I smiled back, reassured, comforted.

I decided to take James's advice. I began to look for other jobs and mentioned as casually as I dared to my father that being a buyer wasn't what I'd hoped, that I didn't really feel that it was right for me. He had already bought the little car, a Hillman Imp which I was to share with my mother, but to my surprise, and infinite relief, he made no protest. He smiled to himself, as if he knew a secret to which I was not privy, and suggested that I looked about.

'Don't hurry it,' he advised. 'And don't give in your notice yet. Say nothing until you're ready to go.'

This sounded sensible and had the advantage of fitting in exactly with my own wishes. I felt a kind of horror at the thought of telling tales to David Eastwell. Much better – and easier – to explain that I was giving in my notice because I had found a pcsition more suited to my talents and disposition. The end of summer sale helped to hold any other kind of drama within the department at bay. We were plunged into a whirl of putting away our best pieces and displaying special sale and damaged goods. The pricing and sorting out took up a great deal of time and Elizabeth Ferrars, who hated sale time, withdrew behind her desk having warned me against disclosing our sales figures to any living soul. It was a quite unnecessary warning. I had no idea what our sales were and, in an unusual fit of candour, said so. She glanced at me sharply and, seeing that I was not being insolent, relaxed a little. I think she guessed that I was hurt by her attitude that I was not to be trusted and she touched my arm briefly.

'Sorry, Marchant,' she murmured, with a touch of her old manner. 'I know I can be rather obsessive. Try to understand. It's not an easy department to run and we're on a kind of continual probation here. We simply can't afford gossip.'

I suspected that this wasn't the real explanation but I grasped it readily, glad to have the least chance of bridging the gulf that had widened between us. I was surprised at my genuine desire to win her friendship but already she was turning back to her desk.

The sale started and, even in our remote position on the fifth floor, all the departments became busy. A continuous, if small, stream of customers found their way up to see what bargains we might be offering. Often we, in the china and glass department, were so busy that Elizabeth Ferrars was obliged to leave the privacy of her desk and come out to assist me. Even Griff was too busy to come prowling round, prying and snooping, to see how we were doing.

I enjoyed the sale. It was a novelty to have so many customers, especially ones who were in such high spirits as they hunted down a genuine bargain and bore it off triumphantly. Before the sale began, Elizabeth Ferrars asked if there were any small piece I might like to choose for myself. I was allowed my usual discount and, at the sale price, a pair of charming Royal Worcester ashtrays caught my attention. The pattern was now out of stock and they were far too pretty, in my opinion, to have ash dropped on the delicately painted flowers. I bought them and gave them to my mother for her birthday. To my delight, and great relief, she loved them and kept them on her dressing table to hold her odds and ends. When she died I brought them home with a few other things that my father was prepared to give up. I have them still, on my own dressing table; a constant memory of her – and of those other far-off days.

At what point did Vanessa decide that she and I were to become models? As I dress for church and later, during the sermon, I am distracted by this question. I think that in those days every young and reasonably pretty girl cherished ideas of becoming a model. The fairytale rises to fame of Jean Shrimpton and Twiggy were ever before us and, when Vanessa saw that a model agency was inviting applicants for an audition, she tore out the advertisement and showed it to me. I think that it must have been at the end of the summer. Tony was buckling down to estate management. His father had been injured in a riding accident and it was necessary for Tony to begin to take some of the responsibilities. James, whose freedom to join our late summer activities had been dictated by harvest and hay-making, had started work at the offices of a company of chartered surveyors and auctioneers in the town. Perhaps it was due to boredom after so much fun that led Vanessa to look for pastures new.

We studied the advertisement together at our table in Mario's. The wording escapes me but I remember our excitement. At first I had no idea that she was including me in her plans. Looking at the small perfect face I could easily imagine her being discovered and whirled off into the glamorous world of modelling.

'You must do it,' I said at once. 'You'll pass. Can you afford it?'

The fee for the course was thirty guineas. It was a great deal of money; six weeks' salary.

'*We* must do it,' she said firmly. 'We'll go together. Think what fun it'll be!'

I stared at her in alarm – but with a rising excitement. 'Oh, no,' I began and imagined my mother's expression; distaste? amusement? 'No,' I said much more firmly. 'I couldn't. Anyway,' this should clinch it, 'I couldn't possibly afford it.'

She looked at me thoughtfully. By now she knew enough about my relationship with my parents to guess that I could not possibly approach them with stories of modelling courses and meteoric rises to fame and riches.

'I'll pay,' she said casually. 'It'll be much more fun together.'

I gaped at her. Even now, with the benefit of hindsight and much more wisdom and common sense than I possessed then, I am quite certain that she was motivated by pure generosity. Even had she needed someone to go along with her, to boost her confidence – which in Vanessa's case is quite laughable! – she had a dozen rich girlfriends who would have considered the whole thing a tremendous hoot. I shook my head.

'How could you afford to pay for both of us? Sixty guineas?' I laughed. 'Honestly . . . .'

'My papa will cough up,' she said confidently. 'Don't worry.'

'But what will you tell him?' I asked anxiously, knowing Vanessa's tendency to fabricate and embroider.

'I shall tell him the truth,' she said, as one who has just discovered a whole new philosophy. She seemed just as surprised at the novelty of this approach as I was. Her expression became almost noble as she considered her new-found virtue. 'I shall tell him that I want you to come with me. He'll cough up. He likes you.'

In an era when it was considered seriously uncool to be approved by the older generation I did not receive this information with any degree of pleasure. I suspected that Vanessa's father liked me because he felt that I would keep her out of trouble. Her stepmother, an ageing expensive beauty, was only too pleased to support anything that kept Vanessa out of her over-dyed hair. Nevertheless . . . .

'You're as bad as James.' She was watching me over her wine glass. 'Drink up and stop fretting. You'll be getting worry lines. I'll go down to the agency in the morning and pick up a couple of application forms.' She looked at the square of paper. 'It's just around the corner from Winslow's. I'll dash out at coffee time. Now what shall we wear for the audition? Think of it! The glossies, television, Rome, New York! Here we come!'

It all seemed quite unreal but I began to feel excited and, when Vanessa's father did indeed 'cough up', I entered fully into the spirit of the thing. After all, I reasoned to myself, if I passed the audition and was given work on the strength of it I could pay him back.

'Of course you'll pass,' said Griff, smiling widely, hands rubbing and rubbing. 'No fear of that.'

I had been unable to contain my excitement any longer than it took for Elizabeth Ferrar's neat and tidy head to descend from view, down the stairs at lunchtime. I was taken aback at Griff's measure of confidence in me. He was not a man given to statements of unqualified approval, quite the reverse, therefore I should have been prepared for what followed.

'Th . . . thanks,' I stammered foolishly. 'But I expect the competition will be pretty strong . . . There will be dozens of girls applying.'

He chuckled, shaking his head, and the smile became a

sneer. 'You'll pass,' he reiterated. 'You'll *all* pass.' I stared at him, puzzled, my excitement fading and giving way to the sensation I often experienced with Griff; one of fear. It was a strange type of fear compounded of several feelings and difficult to convey. It was as if I knew that he was privy to the kind of knowledge that degrades and debases; yet part of me longed to discover what it was that he knew whilst another part of me instinctively shied way from it.

'What do you mean?' I asked and he saw my insecurity, my ready anxiety, and his eyes gleamed.

'It's a mug's game,' he said brutally, still watching me. 'They want your money, that's all. You'll all pass, no fear about that. Won't matter if you've got cross eyes and a dowager's hump. You'll see! Thirty guineas!'

He shook his head contemptuously and waited for my reaction, his hands gently washing themselves all the while, the outward manifestation of his inward delight and anticipation. He had ruined it for me and he knew it. The gilt was off the gingerbread; my excitement destroyed. Nevertheless I struggled to make a comeback.

'They teach you all sorts of things,' I said defensively, wishing I had not told him about the fee for the course. 'Make-up and hair and we have talks by well-known people from television . . . .'

He shook his head at my naiveté. 'You'll see,' he repeated.

I was relieved when his attention was claimed by a customer; later, when he appeared at the entrance to the department, I pretended to be engrossed in some paperwork at my desk. At least I had learned my lesson. I had no intention of mentioning the modelling course to my parents or Elizabeth Ferrars. There was no need to tell Brenda Grice. Griff did it for me. I saw him do it whilst I was dusting the Coalport; heads together, I saw the jerk of his chin towards the department and her quick glances at me. My cheeks felt hot, as though I had been caught out at something despicable, and I hoped that neither of them would come near whilst Elizabeth Ferrars was at tea.

To my relief, the boys were nearly as excited as we were by the prospect of the audition. To have girlfriends that were models would be a most desirable condition and they encouraged us. I nearly mentioned Griff's viewpoint and then decided against it. It might spoil Vanessa's pleasure in the scheme, as it had spoiled mine, and there was no need to risk it. As the boys' enthusiasm grew – Tony already had us on the front pages of *Harper's Bazaar* – I began to feel happier. After all, what did an old fogey like Griff know about it? By the end of the evening I felt much better and, next morning, Brenda Grice had nothing but admiration for my daring and encouraged me to make the most of my chance. I was surprised, assuming that she would take Griff's view of it, but she seemed to be all in favour, encouraging wild flights of fancy whilst Griff stood by smiling to himself.

'By the way,' she said casually, as she turned away, 'my Billy – you know? my husband? – is a photographer. If you need any photographs taken he'd be only too pleased to help. He's got a proper little studio all set up at home. I'm sure he'd give you a special rate.'

I was taken aback – as much at her husband being a photographer as at the kind offer – and thanked her. We had been asked to enclose a photograph with our application but Vanessa had already fixed us up an appointment at a local studio in the town. We went together and were arranged, in turn, in the standard pose of that time; sitting demurely, head turned back slightly over the shoulder, sweet girlish smile. Even in such an unimaginative pose Vanessa managed to look unusual, slightly sexy, arresting. I just looked nice.

'I should like one,' James said, looking at the proofs. 'This one. It's lovely.' He raised his head to look at the original and I felt the usual melting process beginning.

'Fab,' said Tony, Vanessa's proofs spread on the table before him. 'Order me half a dozen. Great. Gorgeous. So when do you start?'

The agency was situated on the first floor of a large old house which was now converted to a shop and offices. Its entrance, I recollect, was through a small door next to the bookshop on the ground floor. We climbed the stairs to the first floor and were ushered into a changing room by a most superior looking woman who stared critically at every new arrival. The audition took place in a spacious room across which stretched a raised catwalk. We sat on chairs placed in two short rows, about a dozen of us eyeing each other covertly, and looked nervously at the catwalk. I remember the terror which struck me when I realised that I would be put through my paces in front of the other girls. Vanessa seemed unmoved, almost amused, by the proceedings.

In due course a young woman appeared – she looked very much like Mary Quant – and in a clipped assured voice explained the way in which the audition would proceed. I remember very little of it now except the terrifying walk along the catwalk which took place at the end of the evening. The Mary Quant lookalike showed us how it was done. She swayed across, eyes narrowed, chin jutting, hips stuck forward, arms elegantly disposed. At my side, Vanessa sat up straighter. This was more like it! One by one we were summoned by that clipped voice and, one by one, we did our best to imitate her. Some marched defiantly; others crept simpering embarrassedly; yet others almost ran, cowering in humiliation. One girl, whose name was Myfanwy, slouched along; shoulders rounded, knees bent, her spotty terrified face hanging down towards her thin chest. Vanessa nudged me. I glanced sideways at her but her face was bland and guileless. When it was her turn she rose confidently and did an excellent imitation of our instructor's earlier performance. There was an absolute silence as Vanessa took to the catwalk as to the manner born; one of the candidates even clapped.

'You were great!' I breathed to her as she sat down again beside me. She gave me another nudge but this time I could see that she was trying not to smile and her eyes shone.

I remember that we were told that we should be advised of the result of the audition by post and we went to collect our coats in silence. The atmosphere in the cloakroom was tense.

'Well, I shan't get in,' said Myfanwy, at last, in a lilting Welsh accent. 'I told my mum it was daft trying even. She made me come, see.'

She looked at us pleadingly, as if apologising for the effrontery of her mother, and we made polite noises which repudiated her modesty.

'I thought I should die,' said a dark girl whose shining hair had been praised by our instructor and who had admitted to polishing it with a silk scarf. The rest of us had sat in silent admiration at such initiative while the instructor had droned on about the importance of personal cleanliness and the necessity of washing one's hair very regularly. 'I felt such a fool.'

These admissions loosed a torrent of exclamations and we all poured down the stairs accompanied by a feeling of goodwill and comradeship. Vanessa and I hurried round to Mario's who – knowing all about it – gave us a drink on the house. We sat at our table feeling somehow different; more worldly wise, more elegant. We felt special, different from the other diners. Vanessa grinned at me.

'You were fantastic,' I said. I shook my head, still amazed by her performance. 'You did it as if you'd been doing it all your life.'

She wrinkled her short straight nose. 'It's just a knack.

- Willa Marsh

And not feeling silly, I think they looked sillier not doing it properly if you see what I mean. No point in being embarrassed about things.'

I watched her enviously. It was all very well for her to talk. 'I shan't get in,' I said but I didn't really mean it. I wanted to hear her contradict me. She did.

'Yes you will,' she said confidently. She took out her lipstick and holding the palm of her left hand before her face, as if it were the glass in her powder compact, she made up her mouth. It was one of her little tricks. She said it was easy but I could never manage it. 'Of course you'll get in. We both will. Not that Myfanwy though,' and she burst out laughing as she put away her lipstick.

She was wrong. We all passed the audition and started the course together. Vanessa and I made various excuses to ourselves about Myfanwy and one or two of the others but, at the back of my mind, I heard Griff's words and I knew that he had been right.

Unable to resist any longer, I climb the stairs to the small boxroom. There in a box in the corner are the remnants of my youth. I work through exam certificates and wads of photographs until I find the piece of paper. 'This is to certify that Fiona Marchant has passed the following . . .' I glance at the top of the certificate. The Richard Deering Model Agency. There were various classes of endeavour and I recall the day when we were finally put through our paces in front of the examiners. One of these was the owner of a hairdressing salon, another managed a boutique, a third was 'someone' from the television, the fourth a professional photographer. We had to model three separate outfits; a daytime ensemble, an evening dress and lastly – rather daringly – nightwear. Each outfit had to have a different hairstyle and we had to change, repair make-up and re-do our hair in the few seconds that would be allotted if this were a professional appearance. I remember that Vanessa advised and helped me through it and that I was just as nervous as though it had indeed been the real thing.

Of course Griff was right. The whole thing was a confidence trick to extort money from vain and silly girls. Within a year the agency was shut and, as I stand holding my certificate, I remember the final sordid little scene which convinced me – if I needed convincing – that Griff had been right all along. The evening after the examination there was a session with the professional photographer, after which certificates were to be handed out. I missed this particular evening, although I cannot now remember why, and, on the last night of our course, I went along to Richard Deering's office to collect my certificate. I knocked and went straight in. He was sitting at his desk; his Mary Quant assistant stood beside him. They stared at me, arrested in their actions, taken unawares at my precipitate arrival in this hallowed place. His handsome face wore the glazed, heavy look of sexual excitement; hers was slack-lipped, her eyes huge. She had an arm about his neck; his hand was up her skirt. I felt the same strange feelings that I sometimes experienced when I was with Griff and, blushing hotly, I stammered something about my certificate. They moved apart then; he riffling the papers about on the desk; she snatching up one of these papers and passing it to me. I fled out without glancing at it and rejoined the others. There was to be a little celebration and someone was pouring wine into tall glasses. The other girls were comparing the photographs they'd had taken at this last session and were giggling and disclaiming over them. I admired these photographs without seeing them and hid at the back when Richard Deering appeared, followed by his assistant, to congratulate us and wish us well. Another illusion had been shattered. How pleased Griff would have been; how he would have enjoyed it.

In the afternoon silence of my boxroom I sigh for the

innocence of youth and wonder what happened to Richard
Deering and his assistant. Glancing down at the certificate in
my hand I notice something else. So worthless was the paper
that Richard Deering had not even bothered to sign it.

12

As I return from my walk and build up the fire, for the early spring afternoon is bright but cold, I think of James and wonder how he is feeling. He will be home with me soon and then our dance will be the slow steps of the funeral march. We know this dance now; we have done it before. First the death of my mother, then Sarah, then James's mother taught us the steps. The movements are sombre and, as we move together through the sequence ahead, our demeanour will be serious, our hearts heavy.

When we were young the autumn was the season of the dance; dinner dances, tea dances, balls. In those days – although the discotheque was becoming popular – it was still essential to be able to circle the ballroom floor without making a fool of oneself. These days only the young dance – or so it seems. I cannot remember when James and I last took to the floor but in those days we were always dancing. Perhaps it was then, in that autumn, that I had the conversation with Elizabeth Ferrars; the conversation I remembered when I saw the rook with a straw in its beak; the day I received Vanessa's letter.

I remember that things were a little easier between us again. Perhaps Griff's attitude to the modelling course had somehow pushed me back across the boundary towards her. I felt awkward with him and avoided him as much as was possible during the six weeks of the course. Brenda Grice remained friendly and interested, asking how I was progressing, what kind of things I was learning. I answered guardedly, knowing that everything would be relayed to Griff, but gradually my optimism and youthful high spirits returned. There were so many exciting things to look forward to and my relationship with James was growing stronger and deeper. I no longer minded going to the canteen. My love for James had rendered Geoff impotent. He could no longer hurt or humiliate me, nor did he wish to; on the contrary, he pursued me steadily for some while. His passion for me grew in direct ratio to my indifference to him and now I went more in dread of pleadings and declarations of undying love than in fear of rejection.

On one afternoon, I recall, I went later than usual, hoping to avoid him, and there, grouped round the biggest table, was the old gang. I was delighted to see them and they greeted me with cries of welcome, dragging up an extra chair for me. I looked round at them; Big Carol, Little Carol, Lorraine, Margaret, Enid . . . .

'Whatever is going on?' I cried. 'How come you're all here together? Miss Tremblett will be having fits!'

'It's Big Carol's leaving tea.' Lorraine's mouth was full of cream bun but she had always been the spokesman. 'We've got extra time.'

I looked at Big Carol. The usual cautious wary look was gone and her face was bright and alive.

'Getting married,' growled Little Carol, making room for me. 'She's going up north. Won't be seeing her again.'

She made it sound as if Big Carol was off to the antipodes. I fetched a cup of tea and squeezed in beside them.

'I'll be back,' said Big Carol but it was clear that she had already gone from us. Her eyes were glowing with the visions of her new life and Winslow's would soon be part of her past. 'I'll come in and see you. I'll buy things from you all in turn.'

We laughed but Little Carol shrugged. 'I'm leaving, too. Got a job with a vet.'

It was obvious that Big Carol had already been told this news but the others cheered and we toasted her with our teacups. We promised that we would all stay in touch and we exchanged addresses but, for me at least, there was an air of finality about the whole thing. Margaret and Enid left the party first and Lorraine sighed.

'It's going to be funny without you,' she said sadly to the Carols. 'It's awful when people leave.'

'You've still got Enid and Margaret,' said Big Carol consolingly. 'And Fiona,' she added as an afterthought.

'It's not the same,' said Lorraine morosely. 'Not with her being stuck up on the fifth floor.' She sighed again as she finished her tea, pushed her cup aside and looked at me hopefully. 'How about going to the flicks tonight? Just to cheer us up a bit.'

I remember how mean I felt when I refused. I wanted to go home and wash my hair and generally prepare for a dance the four of us were going to the following evening. I *could* have managed the cinema but I just didn't want to go. The truth was that Lorraine and the others were part of *my* past now, just as we would be for Big Carol. It was a natural progression. I made some plausible excuse – I cannot now remember what it was – and saw her face fall.

'Perhaps next week,' I began – but she shrugged.

'Perhaps,' she said and the moment passed.

I still feel ashamed of that act of mean-spiritedness. Lorraine had been a good friend to me and I could have spared the time to give her a little of my company when she needed it. Our lives are littered with these tiny betrayals of love and friendship, a reluctance to give of ourselves, and occasionally they return to haunt us. At the time I was simply relieved to have got out of the situation so easily and I went back to the fifth floor, my mind on the coming dance, humming to myself. *'There may be teardrops to shed but while there's moonlight and music and love and romance, let's face the music and dance.'* It had become our theme tune. The four of us would sing it as we returned from parties and balls, huddled together in the big saloon which Tony borrowed from his father if we all wanted to travel together. It suited our philosophy and became 'our' song. We would request it at dances and bought Ella Fitzgerald's record of it. We were the generation who could cross from Count Basie to the Rolling Stones with no difficulty whatever.

I stopped humming as I entered the department. Recently, Elizabeth Ferrars had ticked me off for singing whilst I dusted the Doulton. Even so, it was difficult to restrain my happiness and she glanced at me as I sat down at my little desk. She had become more approachable again and I smiled at her, albeit cautiously. She laid down her pen and looked at me, pushing back her chair a little.

'You're looking very cheerful,' she observed. 'Been offered a rise?'

I laughed. She, of all people, would surely know if that were the case and I did not bother to deny it.

'I love this time of year,' I said, on the spur of the moment, to explain my lightness of heart. I felt I could hardly put it down to the coming dance. It sounded rather too shallow for Elizabeth Ferrars. 'I love the autumn colours and the snap of frost in the air. And Christmas at the end of it. Lovely parties . . . .'

She was shaking her head. 'I hate the autumn,' she said. 'You have a romantic view of it. It's so depressing with the nights drawing in and winter ahead. And generally it's wet and cold. I'm a spring person, Marchant. I need the promise of renewal and fresh hope. I love the early primroses and lambs bleating and the long light evenings.'

She smiled at me. 'You wait. You'll feel just the same when you're older.'

I tried to visualise myself feeling as she did. 'But Christmas,' I insisted. 'Surely the thought of Christmas . . . .'

Her face closed against me, the light dying out of her eyes. 'I hate Christmas,' she said bleakly and turned back to her work.

I sat at my desk feeling rebuffed and foolish and somehow resentful. After all, was it so childish to love Christmas? Later I put the question to Vanessa.

'She's just old, sweetie,' she said dismissively. 'Poor old thing. Must be fifty. Nothing to look forward to at that age.'

'She's not that old,' I protested, feeling some vague requirement to defend her. 'Forty probably.'

Vanessa shrugged. Anyone over thirty was beyond redemption as far as she was concerned. 'Who cares?' she said. 'Dreary old whatsit. What a pity you can't come and work with me in the boutique.'

'It would be fun,' I agreed wistfully.

'Don't worry,' she said. 'Tony's got his eyes open for you. A friend of his is opening an antique shop in Clabber's Close. He thinks you'll be just right as his assistant.'

I was very excited by this news. Clabber's Close was a highly desirable mews in the oldest part of the city and the few shops there were prestigious and jobs were highly prized. I was grateful for Tony's efforts on my behalf and said so.

'Let's hope it comes off,' she said. 'I'll come over and have coffee in the Top Hat. It's right next door. Won't we be posh!'

The Top Hat was a very modern coffee bar. You could have Danish pastries with your espresso and the young pretty waitresses wore black mini dresses, little white aprons and top hats.

'Oh!' I could barely contain my excitement, 'D'you think I'll get the job?'

She considered me appraisingly. 'Don't see why not. Rupert's one of "those",' she emphasised the word, 'so he wouldn't want a terribly sexy sort of girl. You know. All bosoms and haunches and things. You're rather boyish so you'll probably be just right. Tony'll twist his arm. They were at school together.'

I was puzzled by this speech. 'What d'you mean, one of "those"? One of those what? And why wouldn't he want a sexy sort of girl?'

Vanessa looked at me and began to laugh. 'Oh, dear,' she said. 'It's going to be "wanker" all over again, isn't it?'

Even then, some months on, I blushed at the recollection. Even now I feel a prickling of amused embarrassment. How naive I was! I picked up the word from Tony. It was such a *satisfying* word although I had no idea what it meant. 'The man's a wanker,' Tony would say. Or, 'honestly, what a wanker!' There was something almost humorous about it, especially in Tony's languid drawl and I liked the sound of it. I used it and adapted it for my own needs. It was a good way of letting off steam. 'Wanking drawer won't open,' I'd mutter, or 'where're my wanking tights?' 'What a wanker,' I said blithely to Alma when the butcher delivered the wrong order. She didn't turn a hair – not that I expected her to at the time – so I imagine that the word cannot have been in her vocabulary. She was quick enough off the mark to reprove the occasional 'bugger'.

The crunch came when I used it in the car with my parents. 'The man's a wanker' I said loftily, in a fair imitation of Tony's drawl, when a fellow motorist cut my father up and we had to brake violently. My father gave a quick intake of breath, glanced sharply at my mother – whose innocence was a perfect armour – and turned a bricky kind of red. I sensed something was up but gave a mental shrug. Perhaps the incident had really upset him. Later he took me on one side.

'I suspect that you have no idea what the word means,' he said fairly, 'but I don't ever want to hear you use it again.'

I was mystified. 'What word?'

He turned red again; his fair skin, like mine, blushes easily. 'The word you used in the car,' he muttered and, as I still looked baffled, he leaned closer to me – although we were quite alone – and whispered, 'Wanker.'

I stared at him. For a moment I thought he was reproving my slowness, calling *me* a wanker, then I realised what he was saying. 'But what's the matter with it?' I asked. I nearly said that Tony used it but some shred of wisdom bade me hold my tongue. I didn't want him to ban Tony from my list of friends. 'What does it mean?'

'Never mind what it means.' He looked harassed. 'Just don't use it again.'

Once again I felt foolish and resentful, as a child feels when it is castigated for some misdemeanour committed in ignorance. I vowed that I would ask Tony at the first opportunity. I remembered this when we were next all together at a dance. It came to me suddenly and I leaned forward across the table.

'Tony. What does wanker mean?'

He looked at me, taken aback, and then seemed overcome by profound amusement. Vanessa had begun to laugh and even James was smiling. I felt once more like a child, this time with three adults, and suddenly I was cross.

'So what does it *mean*?' I glared at them. 'My father told me off for using it.'

'Oh Christ,' murmured Tony good-humouredly and Vanessa went off into another fit of mirth.

I turned to James who looked repentant but embarrassed. 'It's just ... It means someone who isn't very nice,' he said.

'It does not!' I said, even more cross at being fobbed off. 'It can't mean that! My father was really angry.'

It was Vanessa who stepped into the breach. 'It's all to do with masturbation, darling,' she said, inhaling on a cigarette and nudging Tony who had dropped his face into his hands. 'You know. Doing naughty things to yourself like horrid little boys do. That's what wanking is. Tony knows all about it, you see. He used to do it at school.'

I gazed at her, shocked and suddenly remembered Alma. The blush scorched my cheeks and seemed to suffuse my very eyeballs. 'Oh my God,' I moaned. 'And I said it to Alma. I called the butcher a wanker.'

Tony seemed about to disappear under the table and Vanessa began to laugh again. 'Don't worry, darling,' she said – they'd all met Alma at one time or another – 'your Alma was brought up properly. She went to a *decent* school, not one of these ghastly public schools. She wouldn't know what it means either.'

'Come on,' James was hauling me to my feet, 'let's dance.'

He whirled me away, holding me close, comforting me. Beyond his shoulder I looked back at our table. Tony was sitting with his head in his hands whilst Vanessa leaned against his arm. She was still laughing.

James will be home soon and I must be ready to measure my steps to his. Mine, at present, are too quick and light; happy steps that tap briskly about preparing for a longed-for guest; that lead me away into the past. His steps will be slow and ponderous; preparing to accompany his father on that last solemn journey to the grave. This is hardly the moment to talk about Alex; it would certainly be unwise to upset this new rhythm with any discordant note. James might even insist that we cancel his visit. The very thought sends me hurrying to my bureau to find the letter. With some relief I read that Alex is staying with some school friend on his way to us and will, by now, have left home. It is too late to forestall him. I wonder whether part of my eagerness to see him is to hold off the thoughts of death – Sarah's death – brought close again now. Perhaps it is part – but not all. As his arrival draws near I begin to believe that he will – in some way yet unknown to me – break through the barrier which James's reserve has allowed to grow between us.

I know that his father's death will affect James deeply because it will remind him once again of all the pain and grief we try so hard to contain. The opportunity to talk about this is past, for the moment, and I must be tactful and sensitive with him. I hope that Alex's visit will push us into taking a new approach. Surely Tony's and Vanessa's child, the child of that happy time, of our youth, must bring with him some kind of healing remembrance of those days! In a way he is the child of us all; the result of love and hope and friendship.

I hear the car in the drive and James's footsteps and I go quickly to meet him.

13

James, although sad, is philosophical. He does not, thank Heaven, use the phrases 'happy release' or 'had a good innings' but he talks reflectively on the way in which his father was becoming less able to look after himself and how he hated to be dependent.

'And what better way to go?' he observes, feet stretched to the flames, a glass of whisky in his hand. 'Out like a light. No pain, no suffering.'

I remember my mother's agonising headaches and James's mother's long drawn-out cancer. I think briefly of Sarah – was death instant, as they told us? Did she know nothing about it? – and put the thought quickly away from me.

'How are Philip and Maggie?'

James shoots his lips out consideringly, raises his eyebrows. 'Philip's taking it a bit hard,' he admits. 'Doesn't want to show it, poor old boy, you know what he's like. Maggie's wonderful at a time like this. Quite unemotional. Just gets on and organises it all and those girls of hers are just like her . . . .'

A shadow passes across his face. The spectacles are off, held at arms' length and he massages his eyes. I know that he, too, is thinking of Sarah. Not, as I was, of her death but as she might be now; a little younger than his nieces, less bossy, more demonstrative. She would have comforted him . . . .

'It's such a shame,' I say at random, 'that Philip had no sons. He must wish he had someone to take the farm over in due course. Or maybe the girls will marry likely young men . . . .'

I gabble on a bit so as to carry him over this difficult moment and presently he looks at me and I know that he is himself again.

'I'm so tired,' he tells me and puts his spectacles back on his nose.

He looks exhausted and I feel a pang of fear. It is quite impossible to imagine life without James; the dance over. I smile at him.

'Some hot soup?' I suggest. 'And a sandwich? Something tasty. And a bath and an early night? How does that sound?'

'It sounds like heaven.'

He smiles gratefully at me and holds out his hand and I take it and hold it in both of mine. Our steps are slow, shuffling quietly, but they are steady and sure. I release his hand and leave him dozing by the fire whilst I prepare some supper. Later, he sleeps beside me and I curl into his warmth, unable to sleep. I refuse to let the gloomy spectres of death creep into my mind and deliberately recall the moment when James proposed to me, at a Christmas ball. I found out afterwards that he had spoken to my father on the subject at the end of the summer and my father had told him that he would discuss it again when James had completed three months in his new job. Now I realised why my father had not minded when I told him that I wished to leave Winslow's. He knew that I was not a career woman and that, once I was married, I would want to concentrate on being a wife and mother.

'And what if I'd said "no"?' I'd asked James indignantly, feeling that they had been plotting behind my back, as if they had settled it between them without consulting me.

'You couldn't refuse,' he said. 'What other man of your acquaintance could quote Gerard Manley Hopkins to your mother!' And he whirled me away, into the dance.

It was just before Christmas that Elizabeth Ferrars became silent and withdrawn again. I had begun to see that there was a kind of pattern to these moods but not one that I could chart. She might arrive in the morning in fairly good humour and yet return from lunch, barely speaking. Now that I knew that there was the prospect of the job in Clabber's Close, I could bear it with equanimity but I found myself drawn back towards Griff and Brenda Grice who seemed to be making efforts to be especially kind to me. They were certainly on my side when it came to the question of Christmas decorations.

Traditionally the furniture showrooms had never bothered to decorate but, since the soft furnishings department had opened, Brenda Grice insisted that the whole of the fifth floor should be made more festive. The furniture salesmen seemed indifferent and Griff was actively against decorating until he heard that Elizabeth Ferrars absolutely refused to have so much as a balloon in the department.

'It is a religious festival,' she said coldly, 'and this is a china and glass department, not a toy shop.'

As soon as he heard this, Griff changed his stance. He held by his views that the furniture showrooms should not be decorated – they were too big – but he said that the three small departments could stand a touch of jollity. He insisted that this had been his opinion all along and Brenda Grice and I did not contradict him. We were too pleased to see the tinsel and the balloons going up. It was bad enough being shut away from the seasonal excitement downstairs; surely we could have a little festivity on the fifth floor!

Elizabeth Ferrars watched Brenda Grice holding the steps so that Mr Fullivant could hang paper decorations along the shelving and her lip curled. I knew that she would not relent but I watched the others laughing and enjoying themselves and, when she went to lunch, Brenda Grice carried a plate of mince pies into the department.

'We'll have a tiny celebration while the old cow's off at confession,' she said cheerfully. 'Here, Griff. Eat up.'

He took a mince pie, smiling secretly to himself, dusting the sugar from his dark jacket.

'Does she go to church *every* lunchtime?' I asked. I ate my pie hungrily. It was delicious.

'Has to,' said Griff, eyes gleaming. 'Roman Catholics have to go to confession every day. And she's got more to confess than most.'

'Oh don't listen to him.' She pushed the plate at me. 'Have another one. What about a sip of sherry to go with them? I've got a bottle under the counter.'

'Oh, no,' I said hastily, remembering the effect the brandy had had on Elizabeth Ferrars. 'No thanks. I daren't. She'd notice.'

'You must come round over Christmas,' said Brenda Grice. 'Come and have a drink. Meet Billy.'

'You'll love Billy,' said Griff and he smiled his sneering smile.

He had finished his pie and his hands were rubbing and rubbing. I knew that he was despising Billy just as he had despised Brenda Grice when she had showed off her legs and I felt uncomfortable. She either didn't notice or didn't care for she laughed and offered him the plate.

'You're an old sinner,' she said. 'You ought to be the one at confession.'

He laughed as though she had paid him a compliment and took another pie.

'Yes, you must meet Billy,' he said and glanced over his shoulder as Brenda Grice's boyfriend strolled into the department. He waved to us and Griff raised his voice. 'I was just telling her,' he said, 'that she'd love Billy. That's right, isn't it?'

I was shocked that Griff should mention the husband to the boyfriend and I looked at him, wondering if he would look ashamed or embarrassed. To my amazement he burst out laughing.

'Oh, he's a great guy, our Billy,' he said and nuzzled Brenda Grice's neck. 'Hello, gorgeous.'

She, at least, had the grace to look uncomfortable. She coloured a little and hunched her shoulder against his chin but she was smiling.

'Stop it,' she said but there was a glossy satisfaction about her. 'Give over! What will Fiona think?'

'Oh, she must have a kiss too,' said the boyfriend, as though I were *envying* Brenda Grice and, before I could move, he kissed me full on the mouth.

Instinctively, even twenty-three years on in the darkness of my bedroom, I rub at my lips, shuddering as I remember the bristly touch of his moustache and the whisky-flavoured saliva. I remember that I pulled away from him, aware of Griff's avid eyes and Brenda Grice's watchful ones. I swallowed and, unable to help myself, wiped my mouth on the back of my hand. I knew that it was rude but I simply could not prevent myself.

'You *are* awful,' cooed Brenda Grice at him but there was a brief flash of anger in the cold blue eyes as they surveyed me. 'She's not used to men like you.'

The boyfriend smirked, as though she had paid him a compliment, and said, 'Well, practice makes perfect. I'm sure she'd learn quick enough.'

Griff's smile widened as his glance darted between the three of us and I know that I felt afraid and that I wished that a customer would come into the department.

'I was saying,' Brenda Grice sounded as though she were warning him, 'that she must come to one of our parties.'

He looked at me speculatively but, before he could speak, Mr Fullivant called her away, the men went with her and I was left alone. I was even more puzzled. It seemed that the boyfriend and Billy actually knew one another and that the parties they gave were given by the three of them. I was still mulling it over when Elizabeth Ferrars returned from lunch. It was one of her bad days and I spent the afternoon taking down a Wedgwood dinner service and stacking it on to a trolley ready to go to the dispatch department. I was setting out a Royal Doulton dinner service in its place when Tony wandered into the department.

'My dear girl!' he said, not bothering to lower his voice. 'Vanessa said to come on up. What a perfectly frightful place this is. However do you stand it?'

'Shut up!' I whispered, pulling at his sleeve.

'Terrible mausoleum,' he drawled, gazing round in disbelief. His glance rested on Brenda Grice and Griff, peering at him from across the floor, and Bax, hovering by the lift. He nodded to them regally. 'What a collection of old fossils,' he said. 'Everyone over fifty by the look of it!'

Elizabeth Ferrars had raised her head and was regarding him coldly from behind her desk.

'*Please* Tony,' I begged imploringly. 'Please keep your voice down. I have to work here.'

'Not for much longer, darling,' he said but he lowered his voice a little. 'Came to tell you that the job's yours if you want it. Been with Rupert today and he wants to meet you. Purely a formality. No need to get nervous. Vanessa said to come on up and tell you.'

'It's wonderful, Tony,' I said, edging him towards the top of the stairs. 'Fantastic news. I'm really grateful. I'll see you later.'

'Absolutely! We'll have a celebration at Mario's. I'll tell Vanessa on the way down.'

He glanced round once more, shook his head, and, to

my horror, kissed me soundly in full view of all the fifth floor staff.

'Bye, darling,' he called as he descended the stairs. 'See you tonight.'

Elizabeth Ferrars met me at the entrance to the department.

'I really must protest, Miss Marchant,' she began, loud enough for everyone to hear, 'at your using the department as a place to entertain your friends.'

Now this really was unfair. Apart from Tony only one or two of my friends had ever been up to the fifth floor. These had taken in the hushed atmosphere, the 'old fossils' and the deep gloom that hung about the environs, and had fled, telling me to meet them at some café in the town. I knew that she was referring to my mother's – or rather my father's – friends who had tracked me up to the china and glass department and who swooped round picking up ornaments and putting them down, calling to one another and to me, whilst Elizabeth Ferrars nodded frostily to them from behind the plate glass which enclosed her desk. The problem was that they were all account customers so there was nothing she could do and, after all, they always bought some item, often quite expensive items, and would rush off calling goodbyes.

I swallowed my resentment and apologised. She returned to her desk and I went back to my dinner service. My feet dragged and I knew my face was sullen. I could feel waves of sympathy emanating from the rest of the staff. Brenda Grice went off to tea rolling her eyes furiously and Bax and Griff muttered together, casting sympathetic glances in my direction. Presently Mr Dickson came into the department to say that he wanted to change the window display but needed help to carry the things since his spotty-faced boy was away. Grudgingly, Elizabeth Ferrars said that I might be spared and I went with him gratefully, trying to make the job last until closing time.

'Don't you mind her,' he said, patting me on the shoulder. 'Strange woman, she is. Don't you worry now.'

His kindness nearly reduced me to tears and I avoided the department until I knew that Elizabeth Ferrars was gone. I slipped in and collected my belongings and then hurtled down to the boutique.

'I can't bear it another minute,' I stormed from behind the dressing room curtain, changing as quickly as I could into my new Windsmoor skirt and coat. The skirt was short and straight and the loose swinging jacket was reversible; one side a plain camel to match the skirt; the other a deliciously soft brown tweed. 'Honestly . . . .'

I recounted my woes to Vanessa, not hesitating to put the blame at Tony's feet.

'He was so pleased with himself,' she excused him, 'he just had to come straight up and tell you. He looked quite different when he came down. He said he wondered if he'd wandered into Madame Tussaud's by mistake.'

I laughed with her as she shrugged herself into her coat, a short expensive sheepskin jacket which, then, were all the rage. 'I don't know how I shall face her tomorrow, though,' I added, not *quite* ready to be laughed out of my troubles. 'Although perhaps I could give my notice in if Tony's really sure.'

'Better meet Rupert first.' By now she had explained all about his proclivities. 'And anyway he doesn't open for another six weeks.'

'How can I wait that long?' I groaned. 'I can't bear it.'

Vanessa hunched up her shoulders and pulled a comically dismal face.

'*Soon we'll be without the moon, humming a different tune and then,*' she sang, '*there may be teardrops to shed . . .*' she switched off the lights and we hurried out through the dark store and down the back stairs. Together we sang the chorus, *'So while there's moonlight and music and love and romance let's face the music and dance.'*

I roll over in bed and stretch luxuriously. For a moment my middle-aged body feels young again and full of hope and excitement. Thinking of Alex I fall asleep.

14

I wake early and, unable to doze, I rise and go down into the kitchen. As I wait for the kettle to boil I try to analyse my excitement. Why should the imminent arrival of this boy mean so much to me? Perhaps it is because he is a kind of indirect contact with Vanessa. We have been separated for so many years. She seems close to me again, now, but it is the Vanessa of the past who stands beside me; jigging about on those thin legs and narrow elegant feet, never still when there was music playing; dreamy eyes half closed, as she breathes out clouds of cigarette smoke; lips pouting as she surveys them in the non-existent glass in the palm of her hand. It is the girl of twenty I see, not the middle-aged woman she has become. Her letter and the preparation for Alex's arrival have plunged me back to those days which I thought I had forgotten. No, not forgotten – pushed aside. I think of them from time to time but James's growing reserve and Vanessa's and Tony's divorce had the effect, in some obscure way, of rendering them pointless. It is as if they no longer counted simply because they did not fulfil their early promise; a brilliant prologue to a rather dreary play.

I catch myself up at this point. Surely I do not regard my marriage to James as *dreary*? Of course not! We have been – are! – very happy. His reserve has caused problems but I believe that this has become more apparent since Sarah's death. At the beginning it scarcely existed and I wonder, now, if it was our engagement which changed things a little between the four of us. We were no longer so light-hearted and free. James and I began to take each other more seriously and this must have had an effect on us as a foursome.

As the kettle begins to boil I stare down at the ring on my left hand, turning it a little to catch the light . . . .

'With your eyes,' says James, 'it has to be a sapphire,' and handed me the little velvet box.

For once we were alone. We were sitting, I remember, at a table in a nightclub. We had eaten, although our coffee cups were still before us, and the band – a trio of piano, double bass and drums – was playing softly; 'My Funny Valentine'. Whenever I hear that song, my heart beats fast and I can smell the fragrance of fresh coffee mingling with the scent of freesias in the small vase beside me and the aroma of the cigar being smoked by the man at the next table. A few couples shuffled round on the tiny dance floor and voices were low and intimate. It was to become 'our' place; the place that James and I came to together without the others. The regulars were a little older than we were and none of our crowd ever appeared here. We liked that. We had a privacy to which, hitherto, we were unused and we felt older and more sophisticated.

I pushed my cup and saucer aside and opened the jeweller's box. The blue stone, set in a circle of diamonds, sparkled softly. It was not flashy or opulent and I loved it at once. Heart thumping, I took it from its box; supposing it did not fit? I was so relieved that he had chosen it without me. I should have hated to go into the shop with him, hanging over the trays, wondering how much he could afford. Much better, this way. James leaned across and taking the ring from me, slipped it onto my finger. It was exactly the right size and I gazed at him in delight.

'It's beautiful.' I moved my hand gently, watching the lights in the stone's depths. 'Oh, I love it. How amazing that it fits!'

'I asked your mother if she could sneak one of those silver rings you wear.' He looked pleased, glancing at the ring with pride, delighted with his achievement.

'My mother? And she did?' This was almost as amazing as the ring actually fitting. I simply could not imagine my mother doing anything so – well, so human, so *motherly* as sneaking about and finding one of my rings.

'Well, to be honest, it was your father who actually managed it in the end.' He looked at me ruefully, guessing that the ring would have been even more precious if I could have believed that my mother had been moved to make such an effort for me.

'That sounds more like it.' I shook off my faint disappointment. It had been too much to hope for and I had no intention of letting it spoil this magic moment. 'How clever of you to think of it. Oh, James. It's just perfect.'

We kissed across the table, holding hands, too full of emotion to speak. I gazed at my hand with its unusual burden and James pushed back his chair.

'Come on,' he said.

I followed him onto the floor and into his arms. The dance was slow, dreamy, perfect for this moment. The trio meandered from 'My Funny Valentine' into 'Blue Moon' whilst James held me close and, my hand on his shoulder, I watched the lights reflecting from my ring. I felt safe, assured, womanly, loved. Oh, how happy I was!

'Where did you get that, then?' Griff smiled, hands rubbing and rubbing. 'Out of your Christmas cracker?'

I instantly felt – just as he intended – deflated. For a brief terrible moment the ring lost its magic properties; once again I was young, foolish, uncertain of myself. I even found myself glancing anxiously at my ring, wondering if it did indeed – to other less besotted eyes – look like a cheap imitation cracker ring; a nasty wriggling disloyal doubting of James's taste and generosity that made me hate myself and feel a real anger with Griff. He'd seen my fear and his eyes gleamed and his hands rubbed ecstatically together but, perhaps seeing that flash of rage in my face, he laughed his conciliatory old man's laugh; a high 'heh! heh! heh!' that managed to imply that only an insecure immature girl would take him seriously – and I was unable to challenge him but laughed with him, weakly, unwillingly, furious with my pathetic inability to stand up to him.

Naturally the news went round quickly. Elizabeth Ferrars, to my surprise, needed no ostentatious hand-waving in front of her face to see the ring almost immediately. She examined it, complimented me and wished me happiness.

'Does this mean that you'll be leaving us?' she asked.

Stupidly, I missed a golden opportunity to pave the way for my removal to the antique shop. 'Oh, no,' I said blithely. 'The wedding can't be until next September. My mother has an important exhibition in the summer and she wouldn't have time for a wedding as well.'

It never occurred to me for a moment that my mother should put my wedding before her work. Elizabeth Ferrars smiled a little and asked some questions about James which I answered gladly, always ready to talk about him. For a moment it seemed that we might regain the old friendliness, almost non-existent since Tony's visit, but almost at once she suggested that I change one of the displays from which some stock had been sold and went to sit down at her desk.

I worked quite happily, lost in my own private dreams and looking forward to the celebration that the four of us were to have at Mario's that evening. When lunchtime came and Elizabeth Ferrars had gone, head held high, looking to neither right nor left, a small deputation arrived in the department. Brenda Grice, assessing the ring with calculating eyes, congratulated me with cries of delight whilst Bax and Mr Fullivant made some merry quips and Mr Dickson gave me a peck on the cheek. Even Mr Reed, glad of a genuine excuse to toast someone, raised his hip flask to me and joined in the revelry before disappearing in search of a convenient wardrobe. Griff stood by, smiling. It was almost like the good old times when Elizabeth Ferrars had been away on holiday.

Suddenly Brenda Grice produced a package and a card.

'Just a little something from us all,' she said. 'For your bottom drawer.'

I was very surprised and stammered a little as I took it. They stood round watching as I unwrapped the present, first reading the card which they had all signed. Inside the large flat box, displayed beneath the cellophane lid, was an Irish linen tablecloth in a rich indigo blue with green leaves embroidered upon it. At one end were two matching blue napkins; at the other, two green ones. It was a modern classic, quite beautiful, and I have it still. I was very touched and they looked pleased as I exclaimed over it and re-read my card. Glancing up at them I felt a rush of affection for them all and I reached out to hug Brenda Grice and to smile at the men. They murmured little embarrassed nothings but I could see that they were gratified by my reception of their gift.

They began to drift back to their departments and I went to put the box away in my desk, uncertain as to whether I should show it to Elizabeth Ferrars. I realised that it would be difficult for her to enthuse over anything in which Brenda Grice and Griff had had a hand. I decided to say nothing about it and when she returned I hurried away. Vanessa was waiting for me on the back stairs and we slipped out, not to Mario's this time but to a coffee bar that was in one of the city's art galleries. It was very modern with its tubular steel and glass tables and corduroy covered chairs.

'I've never been here before,' I told her when we'd ordered Scandinavian-type open sandwiches and coffee. 'What made you think of it?'

'I was here the other day with a girlfriend,' she said, 'and I saw something that I thought would make a good present.'

She nodded to a painting hanging on the wall beside our table and I leaned forward to look at it more closely. It is a watercolour entitled 'The Picnic' and shows four people – two girls, two men – seated or lounging on a tartan rug. A hamper stands open beside them and one of the men is pouring wine into the upheld glass of one of the girls. The other man reclines back, a straw hat tilted over his nose, whilst the second girl watches him, a small bunch of wild flowers pressed to her lips. The colours are soft, yet hot; one has the sense of sunshine, the hum of bee, birdsong.

I looked at her. 'Oh, Vanessa. It's *us*.'

She smiled, stirring her coffee, picking at her sandwich. 'That's what I thought. So you'd like it?'

'Like it?'

'Get a grip, darling. Engagement present? Yes?'

'Oh but . . .' I look again at the painting. 'There's no price.'

She chuckled. 'This is an art gallery, sweetie, not the Army and Navy. You don't buy them by the square yard here. Hang on.'

She stood up and wandered over to a desk set discreetly in the corner. The young man in attendance bowed his head to her and, craning my neck a little, I saw that they were leafing through a catalogue. I realised then that this coffee bar was part of an on-going exhibition which sold the artists' work and, sure enough, the young man came across and stuck a small red dot on the corner of the frame, just as they did at my mother's exhibitions once a painting was sold. Vanessa continued to stand at the desk, one heel resting on the other instep, head bent over her cheque book. I had the horrid feeling that the painting was expensive. A closer look showed me the artist's name; one over which my mother had recently showed some enthusiasm, despite the fact that he was a new star in the firmament. Vanessa slid back into her seat.

'He'll pack it up later and send it to you,' she said. 'I told him who your mother is and he's very impressed.'

It was quite impossible to mention the cost of the painting; all I could do was to thank her.

'And if you break up,' she warned me, 'it's yours. OK?'

The suggestion was ludicrous; it was quite impossible to even imagine such a thing. She lit a cigarette, blowing clouds of smoke while I said this, smiling and nodding at my vehemence.

'Great. Fine. OK.' She agreed, accepting my protestations, listening to my declarations of undying love. 'Just hang on to it, darling, that's all.'

I take my coffee through to the study and stare at 'The Picnic' hanging on the wall above the bookcase. It is long since I studied it and once again I am struck by the impression of high summer and the sensation of deeper emotions, disguised by the light-heartedness of the occasion. It is I who sniff at my posy of wild flowers, watching James and wondering what – or of whom – he is thinking as he lies with his eyes closed, a stem of grass clenched lightly between his teeth. It is Tony who reaches to fill Vanessa's glass, debonair as always, whilst she laughs up at him, lying on her side, her head supported by her hand, her wealth of hair cascading down across her shoulder. The whole painting seems suffused with a softly golden light and the faintly distant hills are a chalky blue.

I remember how she watched me across the table, amused by those protestations of mine, and I wonder how she *really* felt when her own dreams crumbled and fell apart. *Why* did she leave Tony, taking the small Alex with her?

'Incompatible, sweetie,' she told me. 'Nobody's fault. And I can't leave Alex to be brought up by nannies. I know what that's like!'

Somehow she made it impossible to question her – or comfort her – and at last I simply accepted that it just hadn't worked out. Yet I was surprised that Tony let Alex go, although I know he has been back to visit him. Perhaps the real reason for Alex's return, as Vanessa put it in her letter, 'to the land of his fathers', is that they feel that it is Tony's turn to get to know his son and train him up as his successor. If it means that we shall see more of him – of both of them – it will be a good thing for us. James needs to get to know his godson; needs to stop using him as a scapegoat for his grief. If only we could *talk*!

At the thought of James, I turn away from the painting and go back to the kitchen to make some more coffee. I take it upstairs and climb into bed. I have grown cold and, as I huddle against him, James turns and draws me down to him, holding me close.

'Coffee?' I murmur. 'I've just made it.'

'It can wait,' he mutters and we move together into the well-known rhythm of our private love-making.

15

James leaves late for the office. Our love-making delays him and he takes time over his shower and getting himself dressed whilst I make more coffee. He is very quiet when, at last, he appears. His face is serious, his gaze inward-looking, and I suspect that he is thinking about his father and decide to make no effort to distract him. I feel happy; relaxed and content and I hold him tightly for a moment before he goes out to the car.

James was my first and only lover. This is not particularly unusual amongst my generation and, although I have occasionally looked at other men and wondered what it might be like to be loved by them, I have never felt deprived of sexual experiences nor that I have 'missed out'. I am boringly monogamous and, since we have been married, dear James has never given me any serious cause for alarm or jealousy. Early on – when I was desperately longing for a child – there was a short period of time when the girl from his former relationship seemed to make a brief re-appearance – I saw them once or twice together in quite innocent situations – but, on reflection, I was convinced that there was nothing to it and I never mentioned my fears to James. After all, she lives and works in the town and I was given to irrational imaginings at that time. It is possible that

James met her accidentally and, since I had made this same mistake once before, I had no wish to raise ghosts from the past or appear to be a jealous wife.

Just after we became engaged, he told me that love-making should be reserved for those moments when one's feelings and emotions are too deep to be expressed by words. Love-making then becomes an extension of those overwhelming longings to show love. That, of course, is true love-making but there are other times within a stable relationship when mutual lust can be tremendous fun.

For us, that came much later; to begin with we were very romantic. It was Vanessa who tried to persuade me that James and I should sleep together before the wedding. I remember that it was a bitterly cold Sunday and that we were in my bedroom. She often came to see us at the weekends. My mother tolerated her; my father adored her. She never felt the need to be polite and deferential as I did with my friends' parents but behaved exactly as she did with me and the boys. She roamed about, picking things up, taking books off shelves, perching on the arm of my father's chair to read the newspaper over his shoulder, wandering into the kitchen to see Alma. To my surprise she won Alma over very quickly. She'd sit on the kitchen table, smoking away, arms folded – Vanessa always huddled into herself as though she were permanently cold – legs swinging, and chat to her about her family. Alma's family, that is; she never talked about her own people.

'So what did Stan do then?' she'd ask. 'I bet old Vera was in a taking!'

She had the most amazing memory for their names and their idiosyncrasies and never failed to ask after the latest baby or a sick member of the family. There was no ulterior motive; she was genuinely interested.

'Just imagine,' she'd say to me later, 'old Alma was brought up in a three-roomed cottage with seven brothers and sisters and an outside lavatory. Doesn't bear thinking about, does it?'

One day she turned up with a parcel for Alma.

'For me?' Alma turned to look at her; her glance suspicious as she dried her hands on her apron. 'Go on with you. What is it?'

Vanessa hitched herself up idly on to the table.

'Just something for the wedding,' she said and lit a cigarette.

I remembered that Alma's youngest daughter was getting married at Easter and that she – Alma – had bought a coat and skirt for the great day. Vanessa had expressed such interest in it that Alma had brought it along one weekend and – bridling – had shown it to us. It was in soft green jersey, second-hand but rarely worn and very smart.

'That's OK,' Vanessa said, taking the moment very seriously. 'That's a really good colour with your hair and eyes. Put the jacket on. Here, give me your pinny.'

Alma slipped the jacket over her old jersey and pretended to model the coat, guying herself up, but her eyes were fixed anxiously on Vanessa. She sat on the table, one leg swinging, eyes narrowed through the inevitable smoke, studying Alma carefully.

'Hold the skirt against you. Yes, that's a good length but you must be careful about shoes, though. It's great, Alma. I really like it. What will you wear at the top?'

Alma looked pleased at Vanessa's approval. She removed the coat carefully, she rarely bought herself new clothes, and smoothed it gently with a red and roughened hand. 'I've got a blouse,' she said a little reluctantly. 'An old one. But it'll do.'

'You need silk with that,' said Vanessa. 'Wouldn't you say, Fiona?'

'Silk!' snorted Alma, folding the jacket and putting it

back in its bag with the skirt. 'Think I'm Rockefeller, do you? Never had silk in my life.'

Vanessa had laughed with her, given her some advice about shoes and promised to lend her a bag. Now, a week later, Alma advanced cautiously upon her present; drawing out the layers of tissue and finally disclosing a silk blouse the colour of rich thick clotted cream. It slipped from its wrapping and, as it slid towards the floor, Alma caught it up. Her expression changed almost ludicrously and she stared at the blouse with a shocked, almost fierce look.

'It wasn't just that she'd bought it for me,' she told me later, 'it was that she actually believed that I had the right to wear a beautiful thing like that. That I was as good as anyone else, if you see what I mean.'

She stood utterly still, the blouse lying across her hands. I saw her pull her lips into a grim line and when she looked up at Vanessa there were tears in her eyes. They stared at one another for a moment and then Vanessa slipped off the table and gave Alma's cheek a quick kiss.

'Pressie,' she said lightly. 'It was just made for that suit. No good fighting fate. Enjoy it.'

She drew me out of the kitchen with her, leaving Alma with the blouse, and we went upstairs and into my bedroom.

'That was really kind of you,' I said, feeling guilty that I hadn't thought of doing something myself. 'Was it from the boutique?'

'Heavens no! The boutique's much too modern for old Alma. I went on a forage to Ladies Fashions. She'll like that floppy bow at the neck and all the fancy bits. So what's new?'

She dismissed Alma and her blouse and went to sit on the radiator, hunching herself up.

'You'll get piles,' I said automatically and we both laughed. 'I'm feeling fed up,' I told her. 'Rupert's decided to postpone the opening of the antique shop until Easter. He's had some problems or other with his decorators. Anyway, it means I can't give in my notice yet.'

'Why not?' She frowned, turning sideways. 'Why don't you take a few weeks between jobs? Get James to ask for some time off and go away together.'

'Go away together? What, on our own?' I imagined my father's face.

'Don't want anyone else with you, do you?' She looked at me slyly. 'Why not just go off and get it over with?'

'Get what over with?'

'The bed thing.' She grinned at my expression. 'Much better to get it over with before the honeymoon. If you leave it much longer old James'll go off bang!'

I laughed, blushing, knowing exactly what she meant. We longed to be together physically. It was awful to separate each night after long-drawn-out kissing sessions that excited us and made us tense. I remember teasing him about his earlier high-minded remark about love-making and he muttered that he hadn't realised how easy it was to run out of words. Vanessa had a point. Sex was becoming too important; it was getting out of proportion and it would have been a tremendous relief to get the act over and done with and be our old selves again.

Vanessa was watching me and I knew quite suddenly that, once again, she was ahead of me.

'Have you and Tony done the . . . the bed thing?' I was too shy to use the proper words.

She looked secretive for a moment and then laughed. 'As it happens, we have. Don't look so shocked. You're as bad as James!'

'I'm not shocked,' I protested. But I was. They weren't even engaged. I longed to ask her what 'the bed thing' was like but, as usual, I felt like a child, shut out from the things that adults did, and I merely asked, as nonchalantly as I could, 'wherever did you manage to do it?'

'It was when we went to stay with William and Georgina,' she said casually – Georgina was Tony's cousin – 'they put us in adjoining rooms.'

I was silenced by the sophistication of her answer. Such behaviour was out of my ken. I sat on my virginal single bed, with my old teddy on the pillow, and watched her with envy and admiration and love. She stood against the huge old-fashioned radiator, arms hugging her breasts, legs crossed at the ankles, head dropping.

'If you want to know,' her voice was muffled, 'it's not all that great. Lot of fuss about nothing if you ask me. Nothing to worry about, anyway. You'll be all right with old James.'

I tried to imagine her and Tony intertwined but my mind shied away from the intimacy of it. I wondered if she wished she hadn't or if Tony had been less keen now that she'd gone so far. For a brief, glorious moment I felt as though I were the elder, the more experienced one, and slipped off the bed and went over to her.

'You may be right,' I said. 'It probably would be a good idea to go away. Of course, I shall be frightened to death. Rigid with fear. Still,' I tried to imitate her casual tone, 'it could be fun.'

She smiled then. 'Be sure to have a few drinks first,' she advised. 'Come on. Let's go down and see if Alma's made a cake.'

'Can you imagine my father's face?' I asked, as we emerged from the bedroom, 'if I told him that James and I were going away for the weekend?'

She grimaced and then shrugged, humming. She seized my arm and we danced across the landing, her voice in my ear.

'*Before the fiddlers have fled, before they ask us to pay the bill and while we still have the chance . . .'* I joined in as we reached the top of the stairs . . . *'let's face the music and dance.'*

I remember that I was too nervous to suggest the idea to James, let alone my father but I *did* take my courage in my hands and go to see David Eastwell.

He looked surprised as I was shown into his office and my hopes that my father might have already dropped a few hints were dashed. He dismissed his secretary and nodded to a chair. I sat down and, stammering a little, began a long, often-rehearsed speech about my inability to look upon being a buyer as the right career for me. Half way through he began fidgeting with his pen. I noticed that he looked tired and worried and his fingers pressed constantly on a point just above his waistline. On the desk stood a glass of milk.

'I wonder, Miss Marchant,' he said, when I'd stumbled to a close, 'if you've given it long enough. You've only been in the department a few months. Barely enough time to start learning the stock. I can understand that it might not seem too exciting for a young girl of your age but the early stages in any career can be rather trying and even boring at times. You'll feel differently when you start learning how to buy. Perhaps we should send you on a buying trip with Mrs Ferrars so that you can see how it really works. I'm sure you'd enjoy it.'

'Honestly,' I began, 'I've really given it a great deal of thought . . . .'

'I'm sure you have.' He stood up, indicating that the interview was ended, and I stood up too, desperate to make my point. 'Please take my advice,' he said, effectively silencing my feeble protests. 'Try it for a little longer and we'll see about that trip to London. Now if you'll excuse me. I'm very busy . . .'

His secretary ushered me out and I went downstairs feeling frustrated.

Of course, it was foolish to have imagined that I could go to see David Eastwell without the rest of the staff knowing five minutes later.

'Been to see your friend upstairs, I hear,' said Griff when Elizabeth Ferrars had gone to tea. He smiled, hands rubbing and rubbing, and I struggled against the power which he seemed to exert over me. He confused me; part of me longing to join him in his whisperings and cruel jokes, to give in and relax and enjoy it; another part rejecting him utterly, disliking and fearing him. Before I could answer, Brenda Grice had come strutting over. Her face was alive with curiosity; her lips smiled with sympathy and friendliness; her eyes snapped, eager and darting.

'What have you been up to?' she asked, all jocularity. 'Has the Old Man had you on the carpet?'

Griff sniggered audibly and Brenda Grice, without taking her eyes from my face, said, 'Shut up, you dirty old bugger.'

I had a sudden desire to be away from them, to run from the building, out into the road, and along to the offices where James worked. I swallowed and then, to my great relief, a customer appeared. She was a regular who must have had a house full of china and glass for she bought quantities of it. I hailed her with relief and saw Griff and Brenda Grice exchange a glance.

'Good afternoon,' I said, and she raised her eyebrows at the exuberant welcome in my voice. 'Your tea set is in,' I told her and she accepted this as my reason for such jubilation.

'I had your card,' she said. 'So sweet of you to get it so quickly.'

'Not at all,' I assured her. 'Come and have a look at it and see what you think.'

I led her into the department, hoping that Elizabeth Ferrars would be back from tea before she left. It occurred to me to wonder if David Eastwell might mention the subject to her, and my heart sank, but a day or two passed and nothing was said. Relieved I prepared myself for my second onslaught, determined that this time he should listen to me and accept my notice, trying, meanwhile, to raise the courage to talk to James about going away together.

As I drive myself to yet another charity fund-raising committee meeting I am still thinking of how all the events conspired together at the end; how I was powerless to stop the machine once it had been put in motion. I remember, too, how Vanessa said to Alma, 'No good fighting fate. Enjoy it.' It was a prophetic remark, as it turned out, though not for Alma – but there was no question of any of us enjoying it.

16

Having been visited by the idea that James might use the death of his father as an excuse to cancel Alex's stay with us, I am relieved when, on checking the calendar, I see that tonight he has a meeting of the parish council. There will be no time for serious conversation. I know that it is too late to contact Alex, nevertheless I fear that the subject might be raised. In the past I have longed for an opportunity to really *talk* to James; to examine our innermost feelings; to understand each other; to comfort each other. Now there is not time to achieve this before Alex arrives. I hope to get through the next few days as quickly and as quietly as possible so that, in the end, James is simply confronted by Alex and then fate will have her way. Is this what is known as 'rushing upon one's fate'? Possibly. How badly she let me down during that springtime twenty-three years ago! Why should I trust her now? Perhaps I feel that it is time she redressed the balance.

If Vanessa had not mentioned it, would I have thought of sleeping with James before our wedding? I might have *thought* about it. Indeed I *did* think about it – and so did he! But would we have *done* anything about it. I think not. Vanessa had roused my anxieties. I had imagined that this act, the 'bed thing', would happen naturally and wonderfully as soon as James and I were alone together after the wedding. The setting would be romantic and exciting and the magical consummation of our love would, in some miraculous way, transform us. We would be officially adult; we would be different.

Now there were doubts in my mind. Vanessa had made it sound rather disappointing; something of an anticlimax. I wondered if this was because she and Tony were not married. James had already admitted that he had an affair whilst he was at university but it embarrassed him to speak of the girl and I tried not to imagine her. They had parted shortly after he started at the agricultural college but I couldn't help wondering if she were prettier or cleverer than I. I tried, no doubt gauchely and transparently, to discover his true feelings about her from his mother but she wisely refused to be drawn and I had to be satisfied with the fact that Mrs Honeywell was obviously delighted that the relationship was over. I longed to be certain that *he* had been the one to tire first; that I was not merely second best. Then, one day, we had met the girl in the town. She stopped to speak to James and my heart sank. She was beautiful; very dark and slim with a bright, eager face. Yes, she was certainly prettier than I and, since she had been at university, she must also be cleverer . . . .

Vanessa attempted to still my fears. 'James didn't ask *her* to marry him, did he?' she asked. 'And it's much better to have a man with some experience.' She said it so firmly that I almost believed her, but I think that I would have preferred to think that James had never loved any other girl but me. 'Anyway, who wants a chap that no other woman fancies?'

I felt comforted but the memory of the girl returned to haunt me. James was very quiet after that meeting and I lived in terror that he might be regretting breaking with her. I longed to ask which of them had severed the tie but pride forbade me to mention the subject. I discussed it endlessly with Vanessa who held that it was evident that James loved me and that it was best to accept that the affair had happened and put it firmly behind us. Alas, seeing the girl had made the whole thing more real for me. There was an easy familiarity between them as they stood laughing and talking together although James had made my status very clear to her. Nevertheless, afterwards I often imagined them together and wondered whether he thought of her. Despite Vanessa's opinions I wished I had been first with him and was beginning to doubt my own beliefs – instilled by Alma – about sex before marriage.

Certainly James's experiences had made him more serious, more responsible, than the rest of us, although this might have been due to the fact that he was older, but I had it firmly in my mind that only within the sanctity of marriage did the 'bed thing' really work properly. Now that I had seen – I must use her name although, even now, it costs me a tiny pang of jealousy – Susie, I was worried lest the act with me might prove so disappointing that our honeymoon and possibly our whole lives together might be spoiled. I strove to be rational; to concentrate on James's love – and his lust – for me. At present our physical desires were out of perspective – I instinctively knew this – and I wanted it dealt with, this 'bed thing', and put in its rightful place within our relationship.

Once James's three-months' probation was up and he was accepted into the company, he found and rented a flat in town. No more travelling up and down each day in the old Morris now; he had his own place and we all felt the magnitude of his new responsibilities. I remember that we helped him give a flat-warming party; the 'bring a bird and bottle' party that was so popular then. The landlord lived downstairs so we were obliged to be quite circumspect but it was a good party. His presence also acted as a restraint on me and James. As I think back to those days it seems quite amazing to remember how inhibited we were. My father warned me against visiting James in his flat alone but it was almost unnecessary. The mere thought of the landlord and his family beneath our feet was enough to dampen even our passion.

Vanessa thought the whole thing frightfully funny. 'But what could he *do*, sweetie?' she asked when I was recounting some incident in which he had knocked on the door one evening when I had gone back to the flat for coffee after the theatre. Fortunately, I was still in my coat but his eyes, darting hither and thither, the flimsy excuse he produced as the reason for his visit, made me feel in some way unclean.

I knew that Vanessa and Tony would have brazened it out, shrieking with laughter when he had returned downstairs, but they were made of sterner stuff. *We* were hedged about with conventions and inhibitions; our consciences were contraceptive enough to protect us – or so we thought.

In the end it happened on a spring night after a party. It was being held at the house of one of Tony's married friends and it had been arranged that we should stay the night. It seemed that all the other guests were staying too. Every corner was filled and when our hostess, with a languid, 'You're engaged, aren't you? Well, you'd better be in here' showed us into a tiny bedroom with a single bed, we were too embarrassed to protest. Tony's friends were the ultimate in sophistication and, pretending that we were quite used to this sort of thing, we let her shut the door upon us. To begin with we were rather shy but we had drunk enough wine to feel less inhibited than usual and soon we were squeezed together into the bed. No doubt we meant to exercise restraint but I was afraid of being prudish and James had drunk just enough to make him reckless. Anyway, we loved each other and I was determined to expunge any memory of Susie from his mind. At some point I remember actually feeling grateful for James's previous experience but, even so, the whole event was rather breathless and muddly and even painful.

James was not prepared for this unlooked for opportunity – I think that, oddly, I was quite pleased that he wasn't; it would have looked so calculated – and I recall my horror when I had to wipe myself down with the sheet, wondering what on earth our hostess would say in the morning. I hardly slept. There was a faintly sordid note about it all that could not be dispelled by simply being in James's arms. When he woke, he got up and went off to find some coffee for us. I thought this was very brave as I huddled the bedclothes round me and tried to feel sophisticated and nonchalant. I looked at my ring, so as to give myself confidence, and worried about the sheet.

'Don't worry,' James said, climbing in beside me with the coffee. 'It was fine. I didn't come inside you,' but his voice was not wholly reassuring and I wished that I had the courage to voice my anxieties, to ask him exactly what he meant.

We sat close together, more like two children than two adults after their first night together. He sensed that I would not be able to relax now that anyone might burst in upon us and he put an arm round me, resting his chin on my head and talking quietly to me. I showed him my blood on the sheet – it was an important moment which we marvelled at together – and he kissed me and we clung to each other feeling that we truly belonged at last. I realised how comforting it would be to be with him like this, calmly and peacefully for the rest of our lives, but I still felt on edge.

Vanessa smiled sleepily at us when she appeared for breakfast. As soon as I could I drew her apart privately and explained about the sheet. She began to laugh and then frowned a little.

'Trust James to muff it,' she said – but tolerantly, as though he were a child. 'He should have worn something. Don't worry about the sheet. Angela's quite used to that sort of thing.'

But I *did* worry about it. In the end I stripped the bed and hid the sheets and pillowcases in the laundry basket in one of the bathrooms.

A few days later James asked casually if I were OK? I asked him what he meant; in what sense OK? After a certain amount of embarrassment he explained the risks associated with *coitus interruptus* and I knew a deadly fear.

'But . . . but you said it was OK. That you didn't . . . you know . . . .'

He broke in hastily with reassurances – but my peace of mind had fled. I imagined explaining to my father – and oh, God! my mother – that I was pregnant. That the wedding was only six months away was no comfort. A baby would be well in evidence by six months. I imagined the gossip if we were obliged to bring the date of the wedding forward and I knew that I would die of shame. I became withdrawn and silent, counting the days off the calendar, waiting for the moment when my period should start. My terror infected James who blamed himself entirely. I tried to blame him, too, but some inner core of self-honesty reminded me that I had been just as eager as he.

I went to the lavatory every ten minutes and started on the 'if onlys' . . . . If only Vanessa had never mentioned the 'bed thing' . . . If only we hadn't gone to the party . . . If only we had been given separate rooms . . . If only James had had the sense to be prepared for such an eventuality . . . If only I hadn't been such a fool . . . .

I talked over my fears with Vanessa at our table at Mario's. She listened, head bent, stirring her espresso, her face thoughtful. She neither condemned nor derided but sat silently, listening as I tore myself apart.

'When are you due?'

'Today.' She raised her head swiftly to stare at me questioningly. I shook my head. 'Not yet,' I said miserably and felt my lips tremble.

'But how do you feel?' she asked. 'D'you feel pre-curse-ish? You know. Irritable and things. Or do you feel sick?'

'I don't know what I feel!' I cried – and glanced round quickly to see if anyone was listening.

'Don't get in a state,' she said. 'That's the worst thing you can do. You want to do something physical to bring it on. Go dancing tonight. Something like that.'

I didn't feel like dancing but I was prepared to try anything. 'What are you doing this evening?'

She shrugged and looked evasive and, through the mists of my own preoccupation, a thought penetrated my tired mind. We hadn't seen Tony around quite so much lately. Our meetings were not quite so regular; his presence not so much in evidence. I remember how I had wondered if he were cooling off and I felt a stab of anxiety and sympathy for Vanessa. It would be quite impossible to ask her what the situation was, so instead I suggested that she and I should go to the cinema. I felt too tired to go dancing and we had both been wanting to see *Doctor Zhivago*. She agreed and we both felt a little brighter at the prospect. James appeared, wearing the faintly anxious look that seemed habitual with him since that wretched party, and I shook my head slightly at his unspoken question. When Vanessa went off to the ladies' cloakroom, I explained my fears about Tony and my suggestion that she and I should go to the cinema. He readily agreed, almost relieved – I suspected – to have an evening to himself, and we spent the rest of the lunchtime each trying to raise the other's spirits.

Back on the fifth floor they flagged again. I felt heavy and dispirited and frightened. I was certain, now, that I was pregnant and I was unable to function efficiently or think intelligently. It was not particularly surprising that I should reach too far with my duster, lose my footing, and, unable to right myself, knock against a display of Waterford goblets. Two fell undamaged to the thickly carpeted floor but three others managed to hit the edges of the glass display counter beneath the shelves and smash to pieces.

I cried out in my distress and Elizabeth Ferrars came rushing from behind her desk.

'Oh, you clumsy child,' she exclaimed crossly. 'Really, this is very careless of you. Whatever were you doing? Go and find a dustpan and brush. Quick!'

I stumbled away, a sob catching at the back of my throat, and saw, from the corner of my eye, Griff hovering, peering to see what all the fuss was about. Elizabeth Ferrars saw him, too. To my intense surprise she rounded on him, asking what he was doing, accusing him of prying. He answered back, his face twisted and sneering, and a full-scale row developed. I stood, astounded, the dustpan and brush hanging from my hands whilst they raged at each other. They seemed oblivious of the other members of staff who moved closer to watch and listen and I prayed that no customer would arrive to witness such an exhibition.

'I shall report you,' cried Elizabeth Ferrars at last, her cheeks bright, her mouth twitching uncontrollably. 'You have spied on this department from the beginning. You question my assistants. I have noticed that, in my absence, papers have been moved on my desk. I shall go upstairs now and speak to Mr Eastwell.'

'Go on then you stupid bitch!' he all but screamed after her. 'Go on then. I know what he'll say . . . .'

Brenda Grice was beside him, pulling him away, muttering in his ear, but he dragged free of her, shaking her off irritably, although he moved back into his own department. She looked over at me and shrugged, rolling her eyes, as if to make light of it and quite stupidly and childishly I burst into tears. She came in to me, clucking and shushing me, and, taking the dustpan and brush from my hands, she pushed me down into my chair.

'For heaven's sake,' she said. 'What a fuss over a few glasses! Tell you what. Why don't you take early tea? Go on. I'll watch the department. It'll be all over when you come back.'

So it was. Elizabeth sat white-faced and tight-lipped behind her glass and Griff was well out of sight, round in his own department. Later I found out that David Eastwell had come down to the fifth floor with Elizabeth Ferrars to find Brenda Grice quietly in charge of china and glass and Griff calmly serving a customer in his own department. He had denounced the whole matter as a storm in a teacup, sent Brenda Grice back to soft furnishings, and, after a few more words with Elizabeth Ferrars – 'giving her a right telling off he was' said Bax gleefully, 'you should have seen her face!' – he returned to his office. She went to tea immediately on my return, head held high, looking neither right nor left, and the whisperers closed in. I felt too shaken to join them. Subdued and silent I crept around the department, longing for it to be five thirty.

I told Vanessa about the row whilst I changed but somehow the usual verve was missing from my account and Vanessa did not react with her ready wit and devastating observations. We had to queue for a seat at the cinema and were glad at last to sit and be entertained. We were rapt away by the story, the performances, the wonderful photography and the music. We watched Omar Sharif, banging on the bus window whilst Julie Christie walked unconsciously and purposefully away from him, and I glanced sideways cautiously at Vanessa, controlling my emotion lest she should accuse me of sentimentality. Shocked, I saw that tears were streaming silently down her cheeks and, her arms crossed, she was hugging herself as though she were trying to contain some terrible pain within her breast.

When James arrives home the languid mood of the morning has dissipated and there is a brittle tone in his voice. I hasten to manipulate the conversation and guide our steps away from dangerous or intricate manoeuvres. It is essential that our movements remain balanced and steady. This is no time for new routines or experiments – and so I take charge; guiding and leading the dance with a smoothness due to years of practice. So adept am I that he is unaware that he is being managed and I feel faintly guilty at my duplicity and correspondingly grateful for his trusting nature which allows it.

I wave him off to his meeting knowing that I can relax at last. He'll go with the others to the pub afterwards and, with luck, the dangerous corner will have been successfully negotiated.

17

Tomorrow evening he will be here! The hours drag slowly by and I am excited and nervous at one and the same time. We have friends coming to supper this evening and I have decided not to postpone it. We have known this couple for many years and I know that they will be tactful and sympathetic about the death of James's father. This morning – I took care to be in bed and feigning sleep when James arrived home last night – as he brings me some coffee he raises the subject.

'You were asleep last night,' he says – and the reserve is there, along with a tiny edge of criticism – 'so I couldn't mention it, but is this the time for a supper party?'

I hastily marshal my wits. By 'the time' does he mean that we should be in mourning? Or does he mean that we need 'the time' to talk about Alex – or rather, Sarah? I am too nervous to make a judgment and fall back on a well-known device.

'I had one of my headaches,' I say, 'and I took a tablet.'

I receive my coffee, managing to look suitably pathetic, but noticing the leap of fear in his eyes.

'Oh, I see. Are you better this morning?'

'I think so.' I frown a little, as though testing myself. 'But I don't want to cancel Margery and Will. They're such old friends and I think we could both do with some light-hearted company. I know it sounds a little heartless but it will do us good.'

'Perhaps you're right.'

He hovers by the door looking so distressed that I feel compunction at my speciousness. I know that I must not weaken, however. If James's reserve should crumble now we might be in no position to cope with Alex. He must come and be dealt with and *then*, perhaps, James and I will be able to open our hearts completely to each other. But not now. Not yet.

'Honestly, darling,' I say gently, 'there is nothing disrespectful to your father's memory in having two very dear friends to supper.'

'No . . .' Still he hesitates and I feel the moment of danger approaching. I use the only means at hand to divert us from taking some disastrous steps.

'Oh!' I spill a few drops of coffee quite deliberately. 'Oh, James . . . .'

He hurries to me at once and I smile, giving him my mug, sinking back on the pillows.

'Are you OK? Is it your head?'

I nod a little, hating myself, and he dabs at the spilt coffee with his handkerchief, pulling the quilt round me, arranging my pillows.

'I'll be all right,' I tell him, bravely. 'I think I could sleep. Do you mind?'

'Of course not. Phone me when you wake . . . .'

He kisses me and leaves the room, shutting the door quietly behind him. Lying tense and still, I hear the front door close, the car engine throb into life, the shush of the tyres on the road. Silence. Releasing my breath, I sit up and glance at the bedside table. To my relief he has left the coffee and I haul myself up and reach for it. Sipping, I think about James and how I love him and how very close we came, once, to parting.

It is frightening to see how even small actions can radically change one's own life and the lives of other people. A thoughtless word, an unconsidered gesture can change the direction in which we are travelling and, looking back, we are hard pressed to remember the reasons or the incidences that were responsible.

Of course, we were under enormous strain. The fear of being pregnant coloured everything I did and, as the days passed, my terror grew and I began to dread the sight of James, that unspoken question now always in his eyes. He tried hard to reassure me, telling me that we could get married at once in the registry office, that being together was all that mattered. Sometimes I was almost comforted but, the spectre of my father's anger – not to mention the disdainful disgust which would be the reaction of my mother – rose to banish any hope of acceptance. He was just as frightened of them as I was; I knew that. He could not hope to carry off such an announcement. I knew that we would all muddle through, somehow, but my heart was weighty with disappointment and misery. For the first time in my life I felt that I was totally approved and loved by both my parents – my mother had actually voluntarily talked about the making of my dress! – and James had been accepted with such wholeheartedness that the idea of shattering their illusions of him – they probably didn't have many about me – was too awful to contemplate.

The time came when I knew that I must give in my notice. Rupert and the antique shop awaited me and I must take my courage in my hands and go again to David Eastwell. Why did I not tell Elizabeth Ferrars first? I was always wary of her, of course. Possibly I feared that she, too, might attempt to dissuade me and I felt too weak, too tired, to confront her. I cannot really think why I simply did not go to the personnel manager. It was he, after all, who hired and fired. I think it was because the job had begun with David Eastwell and that it seemed natural and proper to go to him to finish it.

I made an appointment to see him and, when I was showed in, he got up and came round the desk to me and shook my hand. This, for some reason, unnerved me.

'How are you, Fiona?' he asked – and this use of my Christian name unsettled me further. I wondered if my father had spoken to him, and my heart leaped up hopefully, but when we were both seated and I started on my speech he began to frown.

'I'd hoped,' he said, when I paused for breath, 'that you were going to give us a fair trial.'

Once again I spoke of having no aptitude, no interest; I even spoke of another job which had been offered to me and which sounded much more in my line. He pressed me about the job and, when weakly I gave in and told him about the antique shop, he protested that the jobs were very similar and that my opportunities for advancement were far greater here at Winslow's.

I began to panic and, when I saw that he was actually going to refuse to accept my notice, I abandoned my principles, threw caution to the wind and announced that I no longer wished to work with Elizabeth Ferrars. I told him that we were completely incompatible – I was very proud of that word – and that I had no intention of remaining in the department with her.

Looking back – and I am certain that this is not merely self-deception – I think that I imagined that this was to be between ourselves. Because he was my father's friend I felt that the whole thing from first to last had been, as it were, off the cuff; outside the usual method of employment. I felt that I could approach him as a friend – if a distant one – and that we could deal quietly together. I expected for him now to nod understandingly, accept my notice and let me go. I almost stood up, ready to wish him farewell.

David Eastwell pushed himself back to the length of his arms, his hands gripping the desk, and exhaled deeply.

'So that's it,' he said and he smiled a little, though not at me. 'Of course, we've had complaints before but I hoped that you might be able to cope with her . . . Right!' He sat upright. 'You can leave this to me. I can't say I haven't been waiting for a genuine opportunity to replace her. She's excellent in many ways but quite impossible with other members of staff. It was mentioned in her references but we decided to give her a chance. So.' He smiled now at me and stood up. 'I'm quite happy for Mrs Grice to run the department for a while. We'll see how she gets on. She's wanted it for long enough but her manner . . .' He paused, glancing at me, wondering if he'd been indiscreet. 'You like Mrs Grice, don't you? Get on with her?'

'Yes, but that's not the point.' Fear was filling me. 'I want to leave. Please don't get rid of Mrs Ferrars . . . .'

'Don't worry about it. You're doing us all rather a good turn, you know. I've wondered if she isn't rather unbalanced. She came in here a few weeks ago like a madwoman . . .' He saw my face and patted my shoulder. 'Now don't give it a thought. Off you go . . . .'

'Please,' I said, standing my ground. 'Please don't send her away.' I was horrified at what I had done. 'I didn't mean it. Truly. I just wanted you to take my notice. *Please*.' I was holding his sleeve now, begging him. 'I like her. Really I do. Oh, please.'

Somehow he got me to the door and his secretary hustled me away. I struggled with her, feeling sick, and remembered, suddenly, that I was probably pregnant. It was all too much. Overwhelmed, I tore myself from her grasp and fled down to the staff cloakroom where I locked myself in the lavatory and wept. Presently I pulled myself together and wondered what to do. I longed to run away; to leave and never to go back. Instead, I summoned all my courage and crept back

up to the fifth floor. I barely had time to glimpse the avid
faces of Griff and Brenda Grice when Elizabeth Ferrars
was upon me. Gone was the icy calm; the immaculate
appearance. Her hair was disordered and her face was white;
the mouth stretched uglily, as though she were trying not to
cry. The shock of seeing her so quite deprived me of speech.
It was, in the truest meaning of the word, shocking.

'Why have you done this?' she cried. She ran at me and
seized my arm. 'Why did you say such a thing to Mr Eastwell?
Who put you up to it? We've got on very well. I *trusted* you!
Why did you say you couldn't work with me?'

Horrified, afraid, confused, I lied. 'I didn't say that,' I told
her, trying to free myself. 'I didn't actually say that.' What
had I said? What had David Eastwell *told* her that I'd said?
'I'm leaving anyway. It's got nothing to do with you. I've
got another job.'

She grasped my arm more tightly, her face working. It
was terrible to see. 'Will you say that? Will you come with
me now and say that?'

She was dragging me towards the stairs, oblivious of the
interested onlookers. I was hot with shame and remorse.
I knew that I had done something quite dreadful.

'Please,' I begged, trying to talk quietly, to reason with
her. 'Please wait. Of course I'll come. We'll go together but
please be calm.'

But she wouldn't listen. Mr Harrigan, the assistant
manager, was coming down the stairs and she flew at
him, dragging me with her.

'Miss Marchant says that it's nothing to do with me,' she
cried. 'There's been some terrible mistake. She's prepared
to go now and say so. Please . . . .'

It was horrible. Even in that ghastly moment I wondered
how on earth she could contemplate continuing to work
there having exposed herself so utterly to her enemies.
Mr Harrigan hurried to meet her and, taking her by the

arm, went upstairs with her, motioning me to keep back. I followed a short way, quite unequal to facing the battery of the staff below. He took her into his office and his secretary came out to me. Mr Harrigan had suggested that I took an extended lunch break, she told me. I could go immediately.

For some reason I felt that I must be alone. I could not face either James or Vanessa and so I went to a quiet café on the edge of the cathedral close. I ordered poached eggs on toast but could not bring myself to swallow a single mouthful. Presently I crossed the green and went into the cathedral. Those were the days when cathedrals were still places of worship and one was greeted by peace rather than by a turnstile. I remember that I knelt at the back, beside a pillar, but my prayers were confused and my thoughts unhappy. I was terrified of returning to Winslow's but, at length, I stood up and walked slowly back, climbing the stairs to the fifth floor.

Heart hammering, I approached. Sick with fright I looked cautiously between the shelves towards the big desk. There was no sign of Elizabeth Ferrars; in her place, blonded head bent as she examined the contents of the drawers, was Brenda Grice, triumphant at last. As I reached the entrance the others emerged. Everyone was agog; rumours raced round the department. Elizabeth Ferrars had gone mad; hit David Eastwell; fallen on her knees and begged for mercy.

Griff's smile was exalted; his hands rubbing and rubbing in ecstasy. 'White as a sheet she was when she left,' he reported. 'Mr Harrigan escorted her off the premises. Collected her things looking like death. I watched her. She had to pass right by me.'

How he would have enjoyed it! I knew that he would have placed himself deliberately in her way, enjoying every moment of her humiliation. I felt ill with guilt and shame.

'Well, that's that!' Brenda Grice could barely hide her satisfaction. She and Griff smiled on me; I who had done their dirty work so royally and completely. How well I had played their cards for them! 'Let's tidy up a bit, shall we?' she said. 'I've got all sorts of ideas . . . .'

Later, I went to see Mr Harrigan. He was a quiet gentle man with a limp and I remember that he was very kind to me. I told him how sorry I was; how it had been a terrible muddle. It eased my conscience a little to say that. He was still patently distressed by the scene on the stairs.

'Poor woman.' He shook his head; his mild gaze roaming the middle distance. 'Such a tragic story. I wonder what will happen to her. Her husband is an invalid you know.'

I stiffened. 'No . . . No, I didn't know that.'

'Tragic. He and their child were knocked down by a drunken driver on Christmas Eve. The child was killed . . . .'

'Child?' My voice seemed to come from a long way off; it felt rusty and unused. I cleared my throat and spoke more strongly. 'Child?'

His gaze returned to me and he frowned. 'I should not have told you. She told me once in private so as to explain occasional irregularities in her hours here. Her husband needed certain attention throughout the day. No one else ever knew, that was how she wanted it. Please don't speak of it. Even though she's gone I should hate it to become a subject for gossip. She was a very proud woman and a very brave one.'

I asked again. 'Child?'

He sighed. 'There was a child. Two or three years old he was, I think. After the accident it was found that her husband would never be able to provide her with another. It was a dreadful grief to her. She has to work to support him now.'

He nodded at me, smiling gently, and began to haul himself up the stairs with his odd halting gait.

'Mr Harrigan.' I could barely speak. 'Can you give me her address?'

He looked down at me and shook his head. 'That would be quite irregular.'

'Oh, *please* . . . .'

'It's out of the question.' He spoke with absolute finality.

'She'll be in the phone book,' I said almost defiantly.

He shrugged. 'She used her maiden name,' he said and went on his way.

I returned to the department and sat down at my desk. Now that I had been so useful to her, Brenda Grice allowed me to sit in silence; she even had to remind me to go to tea. I went listlessly downstairs and, for the first time for two weeks, I went to the lavatory simply because I needed to go; my own problems temporarily forgotten. As I reached for the paper roll hanging behind the door I saw the brightness of the blood on my white knickers.

It is early evening. I take the cassoulet out of the slow oven and stir in the crusty beans. The smell is quite delicious. I replace it in the oven to let the other beans become crusty in their turn.

As I have a quick sip at my glass of sherry – I always drink sherry as I prepare the supper – I can remember the overwhelming relief of that moment long ago when I knew that I was not pregnant; the exquisite joy and thankfulness that washed over me. I sat – I recall – for some moments, too limp with gratitude even to be able to stand upright, forgetting Elizabeth Ferrars in my selfishness, until I thought of James. It would be cruel to keep him in suspense a moment longer than was necessary. Some superstition had prevented me from wearing protection after the first few days when my period should have started and I was obliged to go down to the lingerie department to sort myself out.

James was unable to say too much on the telephone, although his relief was apparent, but I wonder now, if we had known the fate in store for us, whether we would have been quite so happy. A child, even one conceived out of wedlock, would have been very precious to us now.

18

I see to it that James eats and drinks well and enjoys his evening whilst Margery and Will – primed by me – stay late, dedicating themselves to keeping James's mind off his grief. They succeed. James rolls into bed and falls instantly asleep. I lie beside him; awake in the darkness. Tomorrow Alex will be here and James, so he tells me when he arrives home earlier this evening, is going down to the farm after work and might even stay the night if he is needed. He mutters things about the funeral arrangements and Phil and his father's will and so on but I know that he is merely postponing the moment when he meets his godson.

I accept all these excuses quite readily. It might be sensible for me to be alone with Alex for a while; to prepare him for James's feelings about Sarah which have caused this antagonism. I hope that Alex will understand. Meanwhile I agree that James must go, give him a large drink and then dance him gently into the *pas de quatre* of the evening. We four are old partners and our steps are practised, easy, soothing. So relaxed are we together that this evening my mind is able to be partially elsewhere. I am still reliving the days after Elizabeth Ferrar's departure.

I searched for her for weeks. I became obsessive. James, once our own drama was over, became irritated by my insistence that I find Elizabeth Ferrars and try to make it up to her. He reasoned with me and even pleaded with me to forget her; but I could not. I kept seeing her face, distorted and so frighteningly uncontrolled; remembering her distress and her humiliation. I imagined – or tried to – her private pain and almost wept with frustration and shame. Sometimes I did weep when I thought of her dead child and injured husband. If only I had guessed!

'How could you have guessed?' cried an impatient James, when I said it for the thousandth time. 'How could you possibly have known?'

I remembered her reactions to abortion, her dislike of Christmas, her expression when I had drunk Tony's brandy. Could I have made a sound deduction from such flimsy data? Oddly, the more James attempted to absolve me, the more determined I was to find her. Even Vanessa became bored with me.

The whole thing came to a head two or three days before I was due to leave Winslow's. I had learned my lesson and this time I went direct to the personnel officer and gave in my notice. To my relief he accepted it and, to my even greater relief, it was not referred to again. For several days I went in fear of a summons to David Eastwell's office but none came and even Brenda Grice made no attempt to dissuade me. My guilt had the effect of making me almost hate her and Griff. In some obscure way I had been manipulated by the pair of them and I felt resentful. Their behaviour seemed so shoddy beside the courage of Elizabeth Ferrars. I tried to reason with myself. When had things gone wrong between us? Was it she who had changed after her holiday – or I? I suspected *then* that to contain such grief as she had known must send one nearly mad. *Now* I know it to be true. How often I have thought of her, understanding now what she must have suffered when her child was killed; run down by an irresponsible drunken driver. At least, when we lost Sarah, I had James to sustain me.

In my attempt to come to terms with my guilt, I sat sullenly in the department, unwilling to join in the general jollity which now pervaded the once gloomy scene. Brenda Grice and Griff drew off from me; watching me carefully, muttering together. It occurred to me that they would be glad to see me go. After all, they had seen my power. I had gone to see my 'friend upstairs' and with what results! *They* might be next on my list. No wonder they made no attempt to change my mind.

On the Wednesday of my final week, I roused myself a little. Lethargically, I began to pack up my things and clear my desk. I came upon several catalogues and wondered if they were of any use, some of the stock illustrated being now discontinued. I looked around to see that the department was empty. Beneath the high windows there was enough space to squeeze into the next department. I had often seen Griff insinuate his lean shape through this narrow passage when Elizabeth Ferrars had gone out. Her desk was placed immediately adjacent to the dividing 'wall' and he would stand, peering at the papers on her desk, hands rubbing and rubbing, whilst he snooped and pried. In the corner there he was barely visible, and he could slide back quickly into his own department, but I had seen him often enough to know that her accusation that papers on her desk had been disturbed was a realistic one.

Now, some instinct moved me towards that narrow aperture. I leaned my head around the corner. Brenda Grice and Griff stood at his desk side by side. Their very attitude lent them an air of conspiracy and I could see that they were looking at something which they were taking care to keep hidden. Every now and then she would nudge him with her elbow and then they would laugh – but silently, furtively – her shoulders hunched, his hands rubbing and rubbing.

Bax appeared at the entrance to the department and they stiffened, she giving Griff a warning jab. She nudged him again, more urgently, and he shuffled the papers and slid them into the half open drawer – body erect, eyes on Bax, only his hands busy – before strolling after her to the edge of the department. Lightly I dropped to my knees and crawled the few feet between me and the desk. Raising my head cautiously I peered into the drawer. The shock wrenched at my gut and turned me quite cold. The big glossy photographs spilling into the drawer were of naked girls; they posed inexpertly for the camera – foolishly, drunkenly, vulgarly – and each one of them was wearing a tiny mask so as to prevent recognition. I stared fascinated at the spread out prints and suddenly I knew exactly what happened at Brenda Grice's and Billy's parties with, no doubt, the boyfriend looking on. I felt sick, seeing again Brenda Grice and Griff exchanging glances, assessing me, and I knew with what ecstasy Griff would gloat over the humiliation and degradation of these silly helpless girls. I realised that my hands were icy and that I needed to keep swallowing and swallowing.

I edged away from the desk back to the aperture and into the department. I felt quite disorientated and my knees shook and I had a horror that either one of them, or both, might come into the department and I might have to be polite to them. I knew that my knowledge would be writ large upon my face and the realisation that I had been their pawn, that for them I had betrayed Elizabeth Ferrars' friendship, overwhelmed me with self-disgust. I picked up my belongings and walked out of the department without looking at either of them. I never went back.

I told nobody; not James, not even Vanessa. I guessed that James might insist that I report the whole thing to David Eastwell and I had a terrible fear that Vanessa might laugh. It might be just another thing about which I was naive and unsophisticated. I simply knew that I could not bear it if Vanessa laughed. I realised, as I pondered this, that it was a long time since I had heard Vanessa laugh. She had been very quiet of late and there was still very little sign of Tony. She said that he was busy with estate management; that his father was keeping his nose to the grindstone but I wondered if it were more serious than that.

That evening at Mario's we were all three very quiet. The images of those photographs superimposed themselves on my inward vision and I felt edgy. It was as though, after that terrible time of waiting and wondering, we were suffering some sort of anticlimax. James was watching me with a kind of irritated patience which annoyed me and Vanessa sat, smoking one cigarette after another, her eyes on the door. She ordered some more wine and James looked at her judiciously.

'Should you drink any more?' he asked. 'How are you getting home?'

'Dear old Nanny.' She smiled at him but the smile faded quickly from her face and she glanced back again, towards the door.

'I can drop her off,' I told him. 'On my way home. I want an early night.'

Indeed I felt exhausted. It was unnatural to keep to myself such a discovery as I had made earlier that day, we had shared everything for so long, but some instinct warned me to keep silent.

'Well *I* don't want an early night,' said Vanessa, pouring the wine. 'For heaven's sake, darling, don't be so dreary. You're like an old married couple already.'

'Better than being childish and immature,' snapped James and we looked at him in surprise.

'Don't be so beastly,' I told him, taking her side, always sensitive when this particular charge was levelled, even when it wasn't at me.

'You're as bad as she is,' he said, hurt that I was siding against him. 'Charging round every lunchtime trying to find this blasted woman. Droning on about her . . . .'

The scene blew up out of nowhere. I cannot now remember what hurtful things we said to each other but it was almost a relief to let off steam and I remember that I tore off his ring, flung it on the table and walked out on them.

The next day I was unwell. I stayed in bed and warned Alma that I wished to speak to nobody. I need not have bothered to issue the instruction. Nobody attempted to contact me. Despite my raging headache and the dizzy spells that assailed me every time I rose from my bed, I was well enough to be hurt and surprised that James did not telephone. We had had one or two arguments before but nothing of this magnitude and, by the time Saturday had come and I still had heard nothing from him, I began to feel frightened.

Alma had telephoned Winslow's and told them that I was ill and would not be back – which solved that problem – and left a message for Vanessa at the boutique. When I rang Vanessa at home on Friday evening, her stepmother told me that she was visiting friends for the weekend. I received a postcard from her on Saturday morning with a scrawl on the back saying that she'd had my message and hoped I was better; but nothing from James. My mood fluctuated between remorse and resentment but I was determined that he should be the one to come to me. I managed to conceal my feelings from my father by pretending to continue to feel unwell – my mother was too preoccupied with her coming exhibition to notice – and I was glad when the weekend was over. I drooped about the house, too afraid to go far from the telephone lest James should ring, but when Vanessa telephoned on Tuesday I was glad to arrange to meet her for lunch the following day.

I caught the bus to the town and it was as I was walking from the bus stop towards Mario's that I saw James. He was with Susie. My misery translated swiftly into a kind of sick terror. I drew back into a shop doorway and watched as they crossed the road together – his hand under her elbow – and went into the pub on the corner. So this was why he hadn't contacted me. Jealousy and pride squeezed my heart and the pain of it caused my eyes to flood with tears. I slunk into the wine bar and sat down in the corner, barely returning Mario's friendly greeting. Vanessa arrived several moments later. She looked washed out and tired and we regarded each other across the checked tablecloth.

'How are you?' she asked anxiously and I felt my lips tremble.

I swallowed hard and she got up and went to fetch us drinks. After a few sips I was able to tell her what had happened; how James had not been in touch and how I had seen him with Susie. She frowned, her eyes fixed on the table, and I drank some more wine. Misery had almost entirely engulfed me and I realised how terribly I loved James now that it was too late.

'Why "too late"?' she asked when I told her this.

I stared at her. 'He obviously prefers her to me,' I said. 'He didn't waste any time getting back to her, did he?'

'It could be coincidence,' she argued. 'He may just have met her in the road. You know he loves you. Don't be so wet!'

'I'm not!' I cried indignantly. 'Be fair! What would *you* do?'

'Phone him up,' she said. 'Phone him up and say you're sorry. You said some pretty awful things, you know.'

I remember being both hurt and surprised. I fully expected her to be entirely on my side. She was watching me. Something in her expression puzzled me and presently she looked away from me and stared down into her glass.

'So did he,' I said defensively. 'I bet *you* wouldn't do it. I can't see you telephoning Tony and apologising for something. Especially when it wasn't your fault. Well, not all of it, anyway. *You* wouldn't crawl!'

'You're wrong,' she said sombrely. 'I've done just that. I phoned him up and told him I was missing him. I went to see him at the weekend.'

I was taken aback by her admission and she glanced at me swiftly and there was something almost desperate in the expression in her eyes.

'I . . . I didn't know . . .' I began and she smiled then, throwing off her strange mood and looking more like the old Vanessa.

'Love's more important than pride,' she told me. 'It really is. James loves you. Honestly. I know it. Don't chuck it away.'

I wanted to believe her but once I was alone again all I could imagine was James and Susie together and my courage forsook me. All week Vanessa nagged me. She talked and talked, reminding me of things that James and I had said and done, urging me to speak to him, accusing me of selfish pride.

'What about *his* pride?' I cried 'Why doesn't *he* make a move?'

'You made it sound very final,' she told me. 'He thinks it's all over, I expect. For goodness sake *do* something before it's too late!'

Immediately I thought of Susie and I was seized with a sick fear. I missed him terribly and, finally, on Sunday afternoon I swallowed my pride and telephoned him. The telephone rang for a long time before he answered it and, when he did, his voice was quiet. I waited for him to take the initiative but he merely asked if I was better. He said that Vanessa had phoned him from the boutique to tell him that I was unwell.

I recall how my heart thumped with terror. He sounded almost indifferent. I apologised for all the things I'd said to him at Mario's and he said that he was sorry, too, but still in that same quiet way. I was really frightened then. The sound of his voice put everything back into perspective. I saw him clearly in my mind's eye and my love for him drove out my fear. I felt calm.

'I'm coming to see you,' I said. 'I'm coming now.'

'It's late,' he protested, 'and you haven't been well.'

'Do you want me to come, James?' I asked gently. 'Please be honest. If you've changed then say so and I won't bother you again.'

He hesitated so long that I felt desperation creep numbingly into my veins and I nearly replaced the receiver.

'No,' he said at last. 'My feelings haven't changed. I love you but . . . .'

'I'm coming,' I said, knowing then how much he meant to me. 'Don't say anything else. I'm coming now' – and I put the receiver down lest he should protest further.

I drove into the town, half wishing that he'd said that he would come to me but knowing that any meeting at home would be fraught with possible interruption. I ran up his stairs, uncaring for once of the landlord, and hammered on the door. He opened it at once and I ran into his arms but, although he held me and comforted me, reassured me of his love, agreed that such a thing must never happen again, somehow things were different.

At last I have come to the root of it; of James's reserve. It was *then* that this slight withholding of himself began. Now, looking out over the church tower, the coffee cold in my mug, I realise that I shall never know how large a part Susie played nor whether he has harboured regrets. I was too afraid to ask, I did not wish to know, although when I saw them together in those early days of our marriage I was struck by a terrible fear. Perhaps he felt that he could never quite trust himself to me again. It was inconceivable to him, no doubt, that I should say such bitter cruel things and hurl his ring back at him. Perhaps I hurt him deeper than I knew. As I lean back against the pillows I can see just how it all happened. We had been so tense for so many weeks, wondering if I were pregnant, and the scene with Elizabeth Ferrars – followed so closely by the discovery of the photographs – was enough to upset a more mature person than I was at that time. I was in a deeply emotional state and I suspect that I used James as a scapegoat for my guilt.

At the time I accepted James's quietness as a reaction to too much emotion. We had suffered a great deal of tension and we needed time to settle down. I started my job at the antique shop and continued, unknown to anyone, my search for Elizabeth Ferrars. I tried every shop and store with a china and glass department and, when I drew a blank, I started looking in other places, too. I wondered if she'd been forced to accept a lesser job – perhaps she had not been given good references – and I found that unconsciously I was always looking for her. I needed to see her, to explain, to apologise. I absolutely required her forgiveness.

Some weeks later Vanessa strolled into the antique shop, waved to Rupert and whisked me next door to the Top Hat.

'I am in pig,' she announced – she was given to these Mitford-esque sayings – and waggled her left hand under my nose. On the third finger was a large diamond solitaire.

'Vanessa! But . . . What . . .?' I was speechless. Only Vanessa would announce her engagement in such a way. I stared at her. The old sparkle was back and she looked jaunty and carefree. 'Does Tony know?'

She burst out laughing. 'Of course, he knows, idiot. He did the proposing!'

'I mean about . . .' I lowered my voice, 'about . . . what you just said.' She could still make me feel gauche and awkward.

'He's thrilled to bits,' she said airily. 'His old mum's not so keen but there you are. Can't win 'em all. So shall we celebrate?'

When I told James later he looked shocked. For once I felt sophisticated and blasé. 'They've been sleeping together for ages,' I told him lightly.

'But I thought they'd split up,' he said.

He looked sombre, even angry, and I knew that he thought that Vanessa had trapped Tony into marrying her; that perhaps she'd become pregnant on purpose. His coolness towards her really started at that time and, when Tony asked him to be best man, he nearly refused.

'But why?' I asked. The wedding was taking place almost at once. 'I'm going to be her chief bridesmaid.'

'That's probably why he's asked me,' he said rather grumpily. 'I'm not Tony's oldest friend. What about those chaps he was at school with? We've only known each other a short time.'

'But it's been such fun,' I said pleadingly. 'Please do it. Do it for me.'

His face twisted a little – he hated being wheedled – and he turned away; but he agreed to it. The wedding was wonderful. I remember the two of them going away in Tony's car in the early summer sunshine. Vanessa stood up in the front of the car, one hand gripping the windscreen, and threw her bouquet to me.

'Your turn next, sweetie,' she called and blew me a kiss as they roared away amidst shouts and cheers, an old boot rattling merrily along behind them. They looked so beautiful, so happy, so *right* together . . . What can have gone wrong between them? Were they, as she said later, simply incompatible? Had Tony discovered it earlier but let himself be persuaded – or blackmailed – back to her? I suspect that I shall never know.

19

At last the day has come and must be got through somehow. Alex is arriving by train later this afternoon and, I assume, will find a taxi to bring him out to us. James was very quiet this morning. I think he accepts that any serious talk must be postponed until after Alex's departure but he looks preoccupied – almost nervous. Of course, he is thinking about his father and the funeral as well as preparing himself for the arrival of his godson; no wonder he looks – well, *distressed* probably describes it best.

He hugs me tightly when he leaves, hesitates as though he is about to speak and then hurries away obviously thinking better of it. I shall not see him now until tomorrow. Once he has gone the day stretches endlessly ahead and there is the tendency to wander to and fro, patting cushions, staring out of windows, fiddling with the flowers. I pull myself together and decide to settle down to some paperwork, writing up notes and so on, and, as I sit down at my bureau, the telephone rings. I know at once that it is Alex and my heart thuds with a kind of foreboding; he has changed his mind and will not be coming.

I snatch up the receiver and gabble the number rather breathlessly.

'Hello.' The voice is cautious, young, slightly unsure of itself. 'Is that Fiona?'

183 •

'Yes it is.' For some reason, his shyness has the effect of eradicating my own. 'Is that Alex?'

'Yes it is.' He gives a little laugh, relieved at being recognised. 'Hi. How are you?'

'I'm well.' I make sure my voice is warm and welcoming. His diffidence has surprised me a little – his letter was so ebullient. 'Very well indeed, thank you and looking forward to seeing you. I hope' I add, voicing my fears 'that you're not phoning to say that something's gone wrong? Have you been delayed?'

'Well, quite the contrary actually.' He gives another little laugh – a kind of breathy snort which betrays his anxiety. 'The thing is . . . I'm here already.'

'My dear boy!' I actually stand up, so genuine is my delight. 'But that's wonderful. I've been wondering how I shall manage to get through the day waiting for you. This is lovely!'

He is silent. Have I gushed? I feel another stab of anxiety. I have no experience in dealing with the young; perhaps I have overdone it?

'That's really very nice of you,' he is saying soberly. 'I . . . I feel rather the same. I caught an early train . . . .'

'I'm so pleased,' I say swiftly. 'Of course James isn't here at the moment but I could easily come and fetch you. Are you at the station now?'

'Yes I am. That would be very kind. Or I could grab a cab . . . .'

'No, no,' I interrupt. 'I'll be there in fifteen minutes. Go into the refreshment room and get yourself some coffee. I'll be with you as soon as I can.'

'Great.' Another hesitation. 'I'm sure we'll recognise each other.'

'I'll carry a rolled up copy of *The Times*,' I tell him gaily 'and a rose between my teeth to be on the safe side.'

Another breathy little snort. 'Yes,' he says, rather inadequately, and once again I fear that I am being over the top.

'See you soon,' I say more sedately. 'I'll come and find you in the refreshment room. Bye.'

I replace the receiver feeling relieved, although my stomach churns with a kind of nervous excitement. I dash about collecting my things and wonder if it is because I am simply not used to this. I hear my friends complaining of being a taxi service for their children and I burn with envy. No doubt I should be just as bored with it as they are if it were part of my daily round, meanwhile it is a delightful novelty and I rush out to the car as though I were on my way to meet a lover.

I have forgotten that Thursday is market day and the journey takes me longer than usual. By the time I reach the station car-park I feel quite sick with apprehension and remain sitting in the car for a moment to calm myself. After all, he is simply a boy – well, a young man. As I sit, taking deep breaths, I try to work out just how old Alex is. A mental calculation tells me that he must be twenty-two, nearly twenty-three; hardly a boy: the same age that Tony was when he married Vanessa. This thought is a rather sobering one. Vanessa and I were both married by the time we were twenty-one; James was twenty-five. Perhaps Vanessa and Tony were simply too young to cope with married life and the responsibilities of the vast estate – especially with a baby born to them within the first year. Neither of them was the responsible type, although Tony took his duties very seriously once he settled down.

I climb out of the car and cross to the station. As I approach the refreshment room I am conscious of another wave of shyness and I enter cautiously, behind a large party of people, hoping to catch a glimpse of Alex before he sees me. I hover behind the group – who are arguing as to which of them should sit down and which should buy the refreshment – and look carefully round.

My heart leaps violently in my breast. James is here! He is sitting in the corner, well back in the shadow. How did he know that Alex was arriving so early? Could Alex have telephoned him at the office? My heart has settled to a steady, harsh bumping. I glance round but see no other young man. No other *young* man . . . Slowly I turn to look back into the corner. James, yes, but the young James who has been so much in my thoughts and memories; James with his bright rumpled hair, a worried expression on his face as he looks at each newcomer searchingly and then stares back at his coffee almost in despair. Grasping the back of a nearby chair for support I watch him . . . and now, at last, I know the truth. I know all of it; I understand James's reserve and why Vanessa left Tony. I know what happened after I stormed out of Mario's having flung my ring in James's face and why James did not have the courage to come back to me afterwards. I know why Vanessa was so desperate to reunite us and how she persuaded Tony to marry her . . . And I know why James avoided her and why he did not wish to be Tony's best man or Alex's godfather. As the facts fall so neatly into place, the shock is so great that I can scarcely breathe.

Alex glances round again, heaves a nervous sigh and . . . the spectacles are off! He seizes the frames between thumb and forefinger and holds them at arms' length, his elbow resting on the table, and massages his eyes with the fingers of the other hand exactly as his father does. This familiar action restores my senses as nothing else could and, when he looks up, I am standing beside him. He pushed back his chair, fumbling with his spectacles, standing up; his face vulnerable and afraid. After all, he is a live bomb come amongst us – and he knows it.

I smile at him. Now that I am close to him I see a look of

Vanessa . . . but, oh, how like James he is. I see him swallow and I sense the fear which his longing, his desperate need for acceptance, has – only just! – overcome.

'Hello Alex,' I say and I hold out my arms for his embrace.

'Maman told me,' he says – and the French word sounds odd on his very English lips – 'when I wanted to know why . . . why Tony didn't ask to see me or invite me to visit. She left him because she felt that it was wrong with the title and so on. She said it was cheating and not fair to Tony's family and he agreed. But I was too young then to know anything and she kept trying to put off telling me.' He looks at me quickly, defensively. 'For *me* – not for her own sake.'

We are at home now, the station being no place for such confidences. He sits beside me silently all the way back but now seems to feel a compulsion to talk. To start with I can sense him feeling his way; wondering how much I know, frightened of the effect he might have, yet driven on by his need to belong.

'Maman says,' he tells me anxiously, 'that it was all her fault, you see. She was determined not to let anyone be hurt . . .' He stops and shakes his head. 'This is very difficult. How can *you* not be hurt? You seemed to know, though. Did my . . . did James tell you?'

'Did your mother tell you just how much like James you are?' I parry his question with another. My feelings are too confused to bear scrutiny.

He nods. 'When you lost Sarah,' he says it tentatively lest the words should be painful to me, 'she sent . . . James a photograph of me with a letter tucked into his birthday card. She wrote something like "it may not be much comfort but you still have a son", and told him the whole truth. But he didn't write back.'

I swallow back my tears and shake my head, remembering those dreadful days. 'It wasn't the easiest time for either of us.'

'No, no.' He is quick to reassure me that he absolutely understands; that the comfort was supposed to be for James, not a request for recognition. 'Maman said that was probably the case. She was already regretting it. You see, she did it on the spur of the moment and then cursed herself for being a fool. She told me everything in the end. We're very close. She's very brave and she's been a good friend.'

I smile reminiscently. 'I can believe that. Will you tell me what she told you? Could you do that, d'you think?'

He nods seriously, considering my request, marshalling the facts as they have been told to him. 'Maman told me all about that summer. She talks about it often. The picnics and the dancing and the song you all used to sing . . .' He laughs a little, carried away now by his story, his eyes inward-looking. He hums a few bars, breaks into the words. '*There may be trouble ahead, so while there's music and moonlight and love and romance . . .?*'

He looks inquiringly at me, eyebrows raised, his eyes amused, and – my gut wrenches with recognition – before me is Vanessa. I nod, unable to speak and he carries on.

'She says it was a magic time, the sun seemed to shine all summer and there were parties and balls and the four of you went everywhere together. She really loved Tony.' His face grows sad. 'Really loved him. I think she still does. She told me about going to see *Doctor Zhivago* and how she wept all the way through because she knew Tony had left her.' I remember the tears streaming down her face and the way she watched the door at Mario's. 'Anyway, she told me that you and James had a bit of a . . . a near miss and everyone was very tense and uptight and you and he had a terrible row and you walked out on him.'

I nod, my heart heavy. It sounds simple, put like that,

but I remember the other factors; Elizabeth Ferrars and my shock at learning about her husband and dead child; Griff and Brenda Grice and those terrible photographs; the terror of thinking myself pregnant. Perhaps when we look back on our moments of failure we should remember all the accompanying facts. It is so easy to tear ourselves apart, thinking that we could have done more, been stronger, more tolerant, forgetting the exact situations we were in at the time. Does Alex truly believe he exists because James and I 'had a bit of a near miss and a terrible row'? I guess what is coming and I steel myself to hear it.

'They drank too much,' Alex is saying. 'Maman was miserable because of Tony and she said that James was absolutely devastated by the things you'd said to him. She was worried about him and stayed with him until he went home. They went back together to James's flat, holding each other up.' He stops, looking miserable, and I touch him lightly on the arm and nod, showing him that I am able to bear what he has to tell me. He smiles and swallows but still cannot quite find the words to tell me that my best friend and my husband slept together twenty-three years ago. 'She says that he kept saying, "but I don't love you. I love Fiona." She says he said it all the way through.'

I cover my face with one hand and try to analyse my emotions. The feeling of pain and hurt is fainter now. It is as if the four of us are one; me, James, Vanessa, Tony, as we were all through that summer. How can we divide one from the other and especially at this great distance? No doubt I would have felt different *then* . . . but *now* . . . I simply feel a great sadness that such magic should fade into muddle and unhappiness. They are not long, the days of wine and roses. I know that he is watching me and presently I straighten up and smile at him.

'She telephoned James and told him that it must be forgotten, that it was a mad drunken moment.' He sees my smile as permission to continue. 'She says he was very cut up about it, so ashamed that he couldn't bring himself to phone you. She tried to persuade him but that in the end he refused to speak to her so she bullied you until you got back together. She was terrified, she said, that she had ruined everything for you. When she found she was pregnant with me she told Tony I was his child. They hadn't been sleeping together for a while – that's how she knew that . . . well, how she knew. But she went to a party and made sure that they were . . . together afterwards. She said that he was still very fond of her and she thought that this was a way of bringing him back to her. She loved him so much she was sure that she could make it work.'

I think of her, standing up in the car, throwing her bouquet and my heart aches.

'Of course it didn't work.' Alex sounds suddenly mature. 'They quarrelled and so on and when she saw how much his lands and his ancestry meant to him she knew she couldn't go on deceiving him any longer. She decided to get out and go abroad.'

I remember how she sat, head bent, thin legs stuck out as Alex played on the carpet at her feet. I know now what she wanted to tell me then.

'She was horrified when you wrote about Sarah. She knew you couldn't have any more children and she wondered if it might be possible then for James to . . . well,' he shrugs, 'acknowledge me.'

His mouth twists in a smile and I look at him quickly. 'Did James know?'

'Heavens no!' He looks horrified. 'When he heard that maman was pregnant he asked her if I was his child and she told him very firmly that I was Tony's. That she was actually pregnant when they . . . when he . . . .'

He falters still over this tricky part and I am quiet, fitting in the small details. It was the photograph that convinced

James, no doubt. He saw himself in that young face. His guilt at having slept with Vanessa must have always contained this tiny fear; even after she reassured him; after I, myself, had told him that Tony and she had been lovers.

'Maman says that he was furious with himself and with her. She fears that he's never forgiven her or himself. When I wanted to come here to study I knew that I wanted to meet . . . James, well, both of you, but I was so afraid that I might be the cause of a great deal of misery.' He looks unhappy. 'I want to meet my father,' he says at last, 'but I don't want to hurt you. I'm so relieved that you seemed to have guessed already.'

He looks anxiously at me and I do not wish to disillusion him. I study him; James's son. I feel no hurt now, nor pain, just a steady, deep, thankful joy. He is the child of that summer; the child of us all; the result of all that we shared together.

'I told maman how I felt and asked her what she advised,' he says, lest I should assume that he had been selfish and taken the decision to himself.

'And what did she say?'

He smiles suddenly, genuinely amused at the recollection, and, once again, with the quirk of the brows and that smile, Vanessa is here with me again.

'She said, "I don't think we can put it off any longer darling," ' he repeats her words faithfully. ' "I think it's time that all of us faced the music." '

20

Early, before Alex appears downstairs for breakfast, I telephone the farm and ask Magda to pass a message to James. I have no desire to speak to him so I give my message quickly and hang up. I say that I am having a bit of a problem and I would like him to come home on his way in to the office, anytime after nine thirty. I give her no chance to offer to call James or to ask what the problem is. By nine thirty Alex will be on his way to his interview and James and I can talk at last.

I spent most of the night awake, mentally writing the script for this talk; a pointless exercise but I could not help myself. By bedtime Alex and I were old friends. He has so much of Vanessa's charm and social ease but at every turn and gesture I see James. He is thoughtful and intelligent but I think – I hope! – that Vanessa's lighter touch has leavened that conscientious weightiness which is part of James's character; that almost censorial uprightness whose unforgiving quality has cast a shadow on our love. If James could have forgiven himself for that lapse, he might have been able to forgive Vanessa and that element of reserve which so often held us apart might never have developed. It is interesting that whilst Sarah was alive he was at his best, his most open and easy. Perhaps he looked upon her death as some kind of judgment; to see the photograph and to learn the truth must have been a very great shock.

During the long dark hours and again this morning I wonder how impossible it must have seemed to him to tell me the truth. To begin with, of course, the truth was only his lapse with Vanessa. I say 'only' now but how would I have reacted then? I can imagine the anguish I would have suffered, unable to believe *then*, with all my insecurity and lack of confidence, that he did not prefer her to me. How ready I was to be jealous of Susie! How could I have accepted that our row at Mario's had resulted in such betrayal of both love and friendship? Would I have been able to see it in the context of all the other tensions and fears? No. It would have been huge to me then; a catastrophe; quite unforgivable. *Now* I am able to imagine them each attempting to comfort the other; their inhibitions removed, their senses dulled by too much wine. To Vanessa it would have meant little more than a generous gesture to ease his unhappiness whilst momentarily forgetting her own. For James the magnitude of that weak moment must have grown greater and greater in his conscience.

When could he have told me? When we were back together again, knowing that our love was more fragile than we realised? On the honeymoon? During those early years when I was unable to conceive? Did his fears arise then to mock him? Had he made Vanessa pregnant whilst I, his lawful wife, was unable to conceive? When else might he have told me? Might he have risked the joy of those happy years when Sarah was alive? How many times has he attempted to bring himself to the starting post, I wonder?

And then, once he *knew* . . . when he'd received the letter containing Vanessa's confession and the photograph, was he likely to be able to tell me after Sarah was dead? What hell he must have been going through during this last week. I realise now how close he has come to telling me the truth and my heart goes out to him. Perhaps I should feel aggrieved and hard-done-by. Perhaps I should feel angry that he has let me face this shock – and it *was* a shock – alone. I feel none of these things. My remembrance of times past has made me see quite clearly how things were. I remember us all as we were then; Vanessa's casual generosity, my naiveté, James's comforting reliability, Tony's debonair charm. The result of all these things – our hopes, our terrors, our laughter, our youth, our *love* – is the sum of Alex. Each one of us had a hand in his making; we are all responsible. No action or word is isolated and we must stand by the consequences.

I hear the car and watch James walk to the door. He looks older – or perhaps it is because his youth is so clear before me – and he looks fearful. This look, this miserable unhappy anxious look on his dear face sends me hurrying into the hall. He shuts the door behind him and turns to face me. We stand across from one another, the spaces of the hall between us, and the silence is absolute. He knows at once that I know everything. We hesitate; each watching the other; testing the old familiar body language. There are new steps to be learned, new rhythms, new patterns, new music.

He swallows audibly. 'I'm so sorry, Fiona.' His voice trembles. 'Are you OK? It must have come as a terrible shock. Honestly,' he shakes his head, 'I just couldn't handle it. I've been such a coward. Please try to forgive me.'

His arms rise a little towards me, although his face is bleak with misery, and the music and the words come sweeping down the years to me and I know that Vanessa is right and the time is come; it is now '. . . *Soon we'll be without the moon, humming a different tune and then . . .*' I remember her dancing with me on the shadowy landing after she'd given Alma the blouse; how we sang together as we fled down the back stairs at Winslow's and out into the sunshine of our picnic lunch; I remember the grey linen dress and the way she put on her lipstick using the palm of her hand as a mirror. I remember how she went abroad, taking the blame and responsibility to herself, and, lastly, I remember the words she has written to me in the long letter that Alex gave to me last night once everything was clear between us. *'We always said we'd share him, darling,'* she writes at the end. *'Your turn now if you want him but let's share the grandchildren, shall we? I'd like that.'*

James is watching me and I smile at him, my hands stretching out to him, and he hurries towards me so that we meet in the middle of the floor, clasped tightly in each other's arms.

'I love you,' he mutters into my hair. 'Only you, ever.'

'We have a son,' I say experimentally, joyfully – but I say it to myself knowing that James is not quite ready yet for such advanced steps – and turn up my face for his kiss. All is well; we are back in the dance.

And what of Elizabeth Ferrars? I searched for her for months, until I was married, and then my failure to bear a child began to obsess me and, as the time passed, the whole affair faded from my mind. Then one day, some years later, I was wandering through a new shop in a neighbouring town – a Guild of Applied Arts – when I saw her. She sat behind the counter, head bent, studying a catalogue. She looked almost unchanged to me, neat and immaculate as ever, her expression still guarded but serene. I watched her for a while and then I approached her.

'Hello,' I said and she looked up at me and, after a moment, she smiled coolly. 'I looked for you,' I told her. 'I looked everywhere. I wanted to apologise. Can you ever forgive me?'

Her smile was a little warmer but her eyes were still wary. 'I'll try,' she said and then, standing up, she saw Sarah in her pushchair. 'You have a child,' she exclaimed and came right round from behind the counter to look at her.

She crouched down beside her and touched Sarah's cheek with her finger. Sarah, thumb in mouth, regarded her stolidly and then, quite suddenly, put out her arms to her. My throat constricted as Elizabeth Ferrars accepted the embrace. She looked up at me and her eyes were suspiciously bright.

'I have a child, too,' she said – and stood up. Her face was proud and I knew a quick spasm of fear, wondering if she might tell me about her dead child. 'I couldn't get another job,' she was saying, 'and quite suddenly we decided to adopt. With all the allowances we were able to manage very well. He's started school now so I'm working part-time so as to earn a little extra.'

I swallowed. 'I'm so glad. So very glad. What's his name? Your little boy?'

'His name is Andrew. It is my husband's second name. He . . . my husband is . . . disabled but somehow Andrew has worked wonders for him. We moved out into the country into a bungalow with a garden and Edward can get about easily in his wheelchair . . .' She shook her head a little, still overwhelmed by the thought of such blessings. 'It's been a kind of miracle.'

'That's wonderful. I . . . I am so very pleased. I felt so . . . .'

'Don't worry.' Her smile, this time, was understanding. 'I forgave you long ago. When Andrew came. ' "Out of evil cometh good." Now we have a son.'

I nodded. Words were difficult. 'So you don't hate Christmas anymore?'

She shook her head. 'Not any more. But I still like spring best.'

I have not seen her since. I have no wish to; everything has been resolved between us. She cannot remove my shame at my behaviour – it is *my* shame, just as James's shame is *his* shame – but now we can see it in proportion, accept it and let it go. We can say, with her, 'we have a son,' and know that we each have a tiny stake in the future. The past is done with, it has gone from us; it is over.

Why then should it be that, each spring when I see a rook with a straw in its beak, I am visited by an inexplicable, unnamed longing; the kind of poignant yearning that one associates with the anguish of youth rather than with the sensible placidity of middle age? It brings with it a memory of picnics, grey linen dresses and dancing; of a special tune that runs constantly, maddeningly, in one's head – and of the bitter-sweet, all-consuming passion of first love.